Champion

Champion

Bicycle Racing in the Age of Miguel Indurain

Samuel Abt

Bicycle Books – San Francisco

Copyright © Samuel Abt, 1993

First printing, 1993

Printed in the United States of America

Published by:
Bicycle Books, Inc.
PO Box 2038
Mill Valley CA 94941

Distributed to the book trade by:
USA: National Book Network, Lanham, MD
Canada: Raincoast Book Distribution, Vancouver, BC
UK: Chris Lloyd Sales and Marketing Services, Poole

Cover design:
Kent Lytle
Cover photograph: Mao, Vandystadt
Frontispiece photo: Presse Sports
Miguel Indurain on the 1992 Tour de France victory podium
flanked by Claudio Chiappucci (left) and Gianni Bugno

Cataloging in Publication Data:
Abt, Samuel
Champion: Bicycle Racing in the Age of Miguel Indurain
1. Sports—bicycle racing
2. Bicycles and bicycling
3. Authorship
I. Title

Library of Congress Catalog Card Number 92-83826
ISBN 0-933201-59-1 Paperback original

This book is for Geoffrey Nicholson, Stephen Bierley and Graham Jones—three of the best—my friends and companions during the Tour de France.

About the Author

Samuel Abt is a deputy editor of the *International Herald Tribune* in Paris and has been closely following the international professional bicycle racing scene since the mid-seventies. His reports from the international racing front regularly appear in the specialist periodical *Velo News*, and he reports on the Tour de France for *The International Herald Tribune* and *The New York Times*.

Beth Schneider photo

Before he moved to France in 1971, he was a copy editor for several newspapers in New England, for the *Baltimore Sun*, and the *New York Times*. A graduate of Brown University, he has also been a Professional Journalism Fellow at Stanford University.

His writings include four popular bicycle racing books: *Breakaway*, published in 1985; *In High Gear*, published in 1989; *LeMond*, published in 1990; and *Tour de France*, published in 1991. In addition, he has edited Waverley Root's autobiography, *The Paris Edition*, to which he also contributed the introduction.

Table of Contents

Prologue: A Sport of Sacrifice and Suffering 11

1. The Lord Indurain **15**
  Building a Champion 23

2. The Challengers **27**
  Up From the Ranks 30
  Too Much Pressure 34

3. Going for Four **37**
  Turning the Heat Up 40
  The Long Road Home 42
  Sprinters to the Fore 45
  Mystery Ailment 48
  Yet Another Explanation 50
  Into the Pyrenees 53
  A Bunch of Hotheads 56
  What the Basques Knew 60
  The Time of the Climbers 62
  Show of Force 65

4. Black Clouds Ahead **67**
  The Picture of Victory 69
  Almost Over 71
  The Final Yellow Jersey 72
  October Again 74

5. Another Tour **77**
  Numero Uno 80
  Off to a Bad Start 83
  Going for the Gold Ring 86
  The Heart of Basque Country 94
  Into the Homeland 97
  A Canny Veteran 101
  An Expert's Analysis 102

6. On the Attack **105**
King of the Walloons 107
Happy in the Yellow Jersey 112
With an S on His Chest 115
Hard Times for Buckler 118
Back in the Broom Wagon 122
No Rest for the Weary 127
Front and Center 129

7. Making the Headlines **131**
The Morning After 134
More Changes of Plans 136
Hampsten's Turnaround 139

8. Rubbing It In **141**
Lanterne Rouge 144
The Winner and Still Champion 148
Getting Ready for the 80th Tour 152
The First Lance 155

Acknowledgements

For their help and friendship on the road, I owe thanks to Louis Viggio, Salvatore Zanca, Phil Liggett, Mike Price, Rupert Guinness, Geoff Drake, William and Alasdair Fotheringham, John Wilcockson and Ian Austen.

For their editorial support, I owe thanks to Christopher Koch, to Rob van der Plas—my editor at Bicycle Books—and to Neil Amdur and Sandra Bailey of *The New York Times* and their caring editors, notably Susan Adams. A big debt is owed to the many reporters of *l'Équipe*, who cover ground no one man can. Special thanks to Laura Leivick, of course. Not least, I thank my children, Claire, Phoebe and John, for their love.

A Sport of Sacrifice and Suffering

The obligation to be modern fuels the disappearance of the old France. "Chic" and "new," the buzzwords of advertising, are used to sell soap, groceries and fashions. In Paris, this is true especially. Paris is a sharp-elbowed city, a city strangled by cars and their insistent horns, a city teeming with people with thin lips and thinner eyes. This great city finds little room in its heart for that which is not chic or new. The vélo—the French word for bicycle—is neither in Paris.

There is Paris and, outside it, there is France.

Not so far outside Paris lies Puteaux, one of many towns where the capital's day laborers spend their nights. On the Rue de Verdun, a hotel advertises rooms by the season: 1,000 francs for the six months of spring and summer, 1,300 francs for the six months of fall and winter, when the cost of heating sends the bill up. The hotel appears to be crowded, with three or four men sharing a room and sending most of the rest of their wages back to their families in Algeria, Tunisia or Morocco.

It is not a very large place, Puteaux, with its rundown charm and low prices and some cobblestoned streets with leaning houses that might have served as models for the paintings of Utrillo.

The town also has an amateur vélo club, CSM Puteaux, and one spring evening a couple of years ago it organized the eighth annual Grand Prix of Puteaux, leaving at 8:15 P.M. precisely from the covered market (open Thursdays and Sundays) on the Rue Chantecoq. In a sweet touch, the club invited cyclists from two of the European towns that Puteaux has twinned itself with, Offenbach, Germany, and

Moedling, Austria. Also in the field of 104 riders were some from the premier French amateur clubs, including CSM Persan, VC Fontainebleau, US Créteil, CC Wasquehal and the vaunted ACBB of Boulogne-Billancourt.

The average foreign tourist has never heard of most of these towns, which offer nothing to see or do compared with the attractions of Paris. They are all much like Puteaux, which, for those interested in history, has little to show besides the 16th-century Notre Dame de Pitié church.

Puteaux is a slow town really, which is why the Grand Prix drew a good crowd on a chilly evening. The route was short, a circuit of 2.3 kilometers, covered 40 times for a total of 92 kilometers including one tough climb and many sharp corners lined with bales of hay. Almost from the start the field was splintered and a group of eight opened a lead of more than a minute. As hundreds standing near the finish line on the Rue Roque de Fillol cheered, Hervé Lépinay, a rider for CSM Puteaux, held off his only challenger, Bruno Lebras of CSM Persan. For Lépinay, this was sweet revenge. "I did to Lebras what he did to me in Paris-Vailly," Lépinay said as he accepted a trophy from the deputy mayor of Puteaux, who arrived just in time to present it and make a dull speech about the virtues of cycling.

Nobody there knew it, but in another year Puteaux would be discovered by real estate speculators, who began knocking down some of the worst houses on the Rue de Verdun and replacing them with high-rise apartment blocks. The gentrification of Puteaux began. Two bakeries were facelifted during the August vacation. Scaffolding began growing all over town and the piano store was scheduled to become a realty office. A vacant lot given over to lilac bushes turned into an office building. Banks opened branches. Paris had arrived at the gates of Puteaux.

Coincidentally the CSM Puteaux cycling club announced a few months later that, because it had lost sponsors in a time of ever-increasing costs, it would withdraw from competition. Presumably this doomed the Grand Prix. In vanishing France, in hoping-to-be-chic Puteaux, there was no protest.

But bicycle racing has roots deep into the French soil. In Paris the preference in sports has moved upmarket to tennis from bicycle racing, which, with its emphasis on struggle and sacrifice, was an ideal sport for a country rebuilding after World War II. Now the mood—in Paris—has turned against sacrifice and suffering.

Only in the countryside, in vanishing France, where the old prejudices live on, is bicycle racing still a major sport. Boulogne sur Gesse in the French southwest is one of those places.

Boulogne is a small town (1,600 residents by generous count) founded by an order of monks in the 13th century. Between then and now not much appears to have happened in Boulogne, according to tourist literature. The biggest day ever arrived on March 23, 1814, when the English army under the Duke of Wellington camped there overnight on its way to fight Napoleon. In seven centuries, Boulogne sur Gesse has produced only two persons judged noteworthy by the same tourist literature: Emmanuel Peres de la Gesse, a minor figure in the French Revolution who advanced to become a baron of the empire, and Jacques Moujica, who won the marathon Bordeaux–Paris bicycle race in 1949.

Moujica is buried in Boulogne sur Gesse, which mourns him still. When the Tour de France whizzed through town a few years ago on a stage from Blagnac to Luz Ardiden in the Pyrenees, journalists with the race were invited to a late breakfast/early lunch—"brunch" is a Paris word—in Boulogne and served bowls of hearty stew and beakers of heartier wine. The reception hall, a market most other days, was decorated with posters celebrating Moujica and his feats. Scrapbooks filled display cases, as did some of his Mercier team jerseys. Townspeople sat on wooden benches with the journalists and talked about Moujica and that *glorious Bordeaux–Paris as if he had won it earlier in the season.*

Outside Paris, where there is little obligation to be modern, where chic and new are distrusted, fans still flock to races to play their own small roles: If the day is hot and a climb long and tiring, people will hold out a bottle of water to a cyclist or pour it over his head. Pushes, even unsolicited ones, may be illegal and yet officials will often look away when a fan helps a faltering climber by shoving him uphill. In the time before a race starts, fans will circulate among the pack, seeking autographs from their favorites, posing for photographs alongside this rider or that, wishing good luck to all. Their grandparents did it, their parents did it and now they do it, bringing their own children. Sacrifice and struggle are still part of this world.

So who could have really been surprised when, last spring, posters announced the next Grand Prix of Puteaux? Any observant eye noticed that the pace of the town's modernization had slowed. The new apartment houses were only partly filled, an attempt at a trendy restaurant opened and closed twice before it became a sandwich shop, vacant stores remained vacant despite their signs promising a bank or boutique. The invasion by Paris had been repulsed and Puteaux was returning to its roots.

One evening in June, the Rue Chantecoq was filled by more than 100 riders from such clubs as AS Corbeil Essonne, VC Levallois and CM Aubervilliers, all towns that no tourist to France ever visits. The field included nine riders from CSM Puteaux, the host club. Had it been resurrected? Or had it never gone away?

Following two motorcycle policemen whose blinking yellow lights announced that the riders were right behind them, the Grand Prix of Puteaux turned a corner and was quickly under way. Long after the riders were out of sight, shouts of "allez, allez," chased them on the evening breeze. Go, go. Go forever.

CHAPTER 1

The Lord Indurain

This was homecoming day for Miguel Indurain. Only 48 hours ago he had won his second Tour de France and now he was returning to Spain, to Navarre Province, to his village of Villava. In the eight years since he had become a professional bicycle racer, Indurain had returned home many times but never quite like this: seated in the back of an open limousine as thousands cheered while he was driven from the airport to the Navarre Parliament.

The farmer's son from a pueblo had become a national hero and Spain was offering him tribute once again. After Indurain's first victory in the Tour the year before—only the fourth for a Spaniard since the race began in 1903—he was welcomed home to a day and night of fiesta by 15,000 people, more than double the size of his village. This time the crowds were even larger, for he had won not only the Tour again but also the Giro d'Italia in the same year. In 1991 he returned home in a helicopter before going to address the Navarre Parliament; in 1992 nothing less than a motorcade would do.

At the Parliament he was handed a microphone and, as a huge crowd chanted his name, he spoke simply. "My triumph is yours," he said. "I want to share it with you to thank you for all the passion you have always shown me." Indurain held out one of the leader's yellow jerseys that he had won in the Tour. "I offer this yellow jersey, the symbol of my victory, to the president of our government. It belongs to all of you too. Forever."

Homecoming day was just starting and, in the words of Cervantes, Indurain was "a king by (his) own fireside as much as any monarch on his throne." After lunch with his family at their farmhouse he went to the Pamplona apartment of his fiancée, Marisa López de Goicoechea, to rest before returning to Villava early in the evening.

Indurain was back in the limousine as it traveled to the Plaza Miguel Indurain where a choir sang a hymn composed in his honor. Off he went next to his boyhood church, as he had the year before, to pray and leave flowers at the statue of the Virgin of Rosario in thanks. The rest of the night was spent at a hall where fans celebrated him and his victory with wine, food and song. Throughout, although he was the center of attention, Indurain kept slipping into the crowd, toward the back, away from the clamor. His smile of pleasure hinted at a certain disbelief, although that might have been shyness.

In a chivalrous age Miguel Indurain would be the parfait knight: pure, serene, untroubled by second thoughts. He has won the Tour de France, the world's most demanding bicycle race—and probably sports event—twice and there is no reason to doubt he can win it again. Ask him how many Tours he thinks he can win and he replies, "Several." But he doubts that he can equal the record of five held by Jacques Anquetil, Eddy Merckx and Bernard Hinault. "No," he said early in 1992, "because I give myself only four more years in the sport, five at the most. So I'd have to win every year or almost every year, and that seems impossible. I won my first Tour when I was 27, a little late."

He might have won a third Tour already but sacrificed his chances in 1990 for the sake of team strategy. He was uncomplaining. "Win or lose, I try to remain the same person," Indurain said after his first Tour victory. "I'm proud of what I've done in the Tour but you have to keep your perspective. It's just a bicycle race, after all."

Nobody can quite explain why Indurain is so dominant. His directeur sportif with the Banesto team from his native Spain thinks the secret is his height. Indurain measures 1.88 meters (6 foot 2 inches) and 80 kilograms (176 pounds), both figures abnormally large for a star climber.

"It's the length of his femur," his thighbone, says the directeur sportif, José-Miguel Echavarri. "Because of his build, his legs provide more power than other riders can generate." Opponents point to other physical gifts. "Indurain has a lung capacity of 6.9 liters, and if you have ever seen photos of him, you will have noticed how his stomach protrudes as he rides," wrote Allan Peiper of the Tulip team in *VeloNews*. "His lungs take up so much space in his torso that his intestinal tract is pushed out to give more room to his lungs to open fully."

Other opponents are not so scientific in their observations. "He's an extraterrestrial," declared Gianni Bugno after Indurain humiliated him, and the rest of the pack, in a time trial in the 1992 Tour. "I thought I was riding well, really strong, but I kept losing time to him every kilometer," complained Greg LeMond after the same time trial. "It was unreal and I can't explain it."

Indurain cannot either. Or, if he can, he chooses not to. After his easy victory in the 1992 Giro d'Italia, Indurain told how he hoped to win the Tour de France. The strategy was the same one he used in the Giro and it was simple: Stay with the best climbers in the mountains and pulverize them in the time trials.

"It's classic," said the American rider Andy Hampsten. "But it isn't easy. He makes it look easy."

But only on the bicycle. Indurain is a tough interview, as they say in the trade, replying to questions in generalities and cliches when he replies at all. "Even the woman of his life, 20 years from now, will not know with whom she has spent her nights," complained a Madrid journalist in print a few years back. Indurain is so placid that on the rare exceptions that he shows a sign of temper, it makes news. In the 1992 Tour, a rider from another team stepped on his feet as he was changing shoes after a stage. In pain, Indurain yelled at him and wound up in the headlines. The only other known occasion of an outburst—if that is the word—occurred several years ago when, badgered by Spanish reporters, Indurain casually offered them that universal sign of dismissal, an upraised right arm gripped over the elbow by the left hand. The reporters tripped on each other to file reports that he was capable of such a rude gesture.

He smiles a lot and acts friendly but relies on Banesto teammates and officials to translate his Spanish and flesh out his answers. His younger brother Prudencio, who also rides, without distinction, for Banesto, often signs autographs for both of them.

Indurain never boasts. By custom, a Spanish winner of the Tour gives the leader's yellow jersey to the king. When his Banesto team met with King Juan Carlos at his palace in 1991, the king went directly to Pedro Delgado to compliment him on his victory. "Not this time, Your Majesty," said the winner of the 1988 Tour. "This time, it's him." Delgado pointed to Indurain, standing back among the rest of the team.

His modesty extends even to competition. The man who knows him best, Echavarri, explains it this way: "I've known only one other rider able to dominate the way Indurain does and that was Eddy Merckx. But Merckx was a robot and his force humiliated his opponents. Miguel is a lord. He's generous and respects his opponents." Echavarri named four riders who won stages in the 1992 Giro. "They know they won because Miguel held back and let them win. Two of them came around and thanked him afterward."

Indurain looks fast in a race. He does not sway on his bicycle as most others do toward the end of a long time trial and he usually climbs with his mouth closed, instead of open and gasping for breath. "Everybody tells me that I never look as if I'm suffering," Indurain says. "But, when I watch videotapes of a race, I always remember the pain I had to endure."

"His pants are never dirty because he never works up a sweat and has to wipe his hands on his pants," says Peiper. "He always looks like he's riding down the Champs-Élysées. His shorts are never dirty, his hat is always in the same position, there's never a hair out of place.

"That's because he never gets to the point where he has to sweat until he's up in the mountains. He's never really put under pressure till about 95 percent of us aren't there any more." It took a while to get to this point: Indurain began riding the Tour de France in 1985, his first year as a professional, and quit after the fourth of 21 stages. He quit in the 12th stage the next year. Thereafter his final places started modestly with a 97th in 1987, a 47th in 1988, a 17th in 1989, a 10th in 1990 and then his two successive victories. Similarly, his record of major victories outside the Tour shows an upward progression: the Tour of the European Community (formerly the Tour de l'Avenir) in 1986, the Tour of Catalonia in 1988, Paris–Nice and the Critérium International in 1989, Paris–Nice and the Grand Prix de Saint Sebastián in 1990. He won his first stage in the Tour in 1989 and has added six since then.

Despite his great success, Indurain does not seem to be especially dedicated to bicycle racing. He refuses, for example, to try to break the world record for the hour's ride against the clock although, in the final time trial of the 1992 Tour, he exceeded by more than a kilometer Francesco Moser's record of 51.151 kilometers an hour (32 mph). No time, no interest, Indurain explains.

"I live for cycling, yes," he told the Belgian journalist Noël Truyers in 1992, "but it's not a vocation. I'm in the sport to succeed in life. That's my motivation. Without cycling, I would have made a living too. The bike is no necessity. Suppose I have a very bad fall next season and my career is over. I'll regret that, of course, but I'll survive."

He is in the classic mold of the European who turns to bicycle racing to better himself, to escape from the farm, factory or mine. "It's a way of getting out of a certain environment, of knowing another life," Indurain agrees. Although he makes about $1.75 million a year in salary, probably another $1 million in endorsements and is a partner in a big sporting goods store in Spain, Indurain long lived with his parents, brother and three sisters—Isabel, a year older than Miguel and the oldest of the children, María Dolores and María Asuncion—in his childhood house on the small family farm (wheat and chickens). He moved out, of course, after his marriage in November 1992 and a short honeymoon in Florida. As Indurain says, he does not like to travel and he does not like to spend too many days on vacation, away from his heavy training schedule.

He and his bride still live in Navarre province, which adjoins the Basque provinces of Spain. As a Spanish journalist explained after Indurain's victory in the 1991 Tour: "To most Spaniards, he is a Basque. To the Basques, he is a Spaniard, except that he becomes a Basque when he wins the Tour de France." (Indurain has his own formula: "I was born in Navarre and have a Spanish passport. But above all I'm a bicycle racer.")

Whatever, he has at least two dates to celebrate during each Tour. The first is the feast of San Fermín, the patron saint of Pamplona, where bulls are set running in his honor. The feast continues for a week, and the Banesto team traditionally wears red neckerchiefs to honor San Fermín and Indurain. The second big day is his birthday, July 16. He will turn 29 in 1993.

His first sport was soccer, which he played at school. He began bicycle racing at age 11 and admits that a major motivation was the ham sandwich and soft drink that were given to finishers. Quickly discouraged, he gave up racing and returned to soccer. "I didn't like the team mentality, though," he recalled for Truyers. "I wanted an individual sport, so I changed once more. This time, I did some track and field, and started running the 400 meters, even becoming the district champion. But cycling was always in my head, so I started again when I was 16." His first victory as an amateur occurred in the Spanish championships in 1983. "Nobody knew me until then. I remember the newspaper the next day, they didn't even spell my name right." (For the record, it is Miguel Angel Indurain-Larraya.)

Everybody in Spain knows him now. He was asked to carry the Olympic flame on the last leg to Montjuich stadium in Barcelona for the 1992 Summer Games and had to decline only because the date of the opening ceremony clashed with the last stage of the Tour in Paris. Even an offer by the Olympic organizers to fly him down and back in a private plane could not change his mind. When he did get to the Games, to watch the demonstration sport of Basque pelota, he was mobbed.

For that popularity and his success as a rider, Indurain has willingly made sacrifices. "You have to know what you want in life," he says. "I race to become always stronger, always better, to get better results. So I make sacrifices. I live a strict life. Lots of things interest me but I don't have the right to let them get mixed up with my racing. Later, when I've finished racing, I'll make time for them."

Spaniards have usually excelled as climbers, a discipline in which Indurain has few close rivals even if he is not regarded as a pure climber—which is to say a rider who cannot do much more than climb. His true strength is the time trial, that most demanding of all disciplines in professional bicycle racing.

The time trial is simply a race against the clock, with each rider leaving at regular intervals in inverse order of ranking. Cooperation is banned: No relays may be offered or accepted. The ideal time trialist is a legendary fellow—the French say he's Belgian, the Belgians say he's Dutch, the Dutch say he's French—who has no head for strategy. In a time trial, his only instructions are "Faster, faster." That is not quite fair to Indurain, but not quite unfair either.

What the ideal time trialist really needs is concentration, which the Spaniard possesses, a sense of tunnel vision for a constant 20 or 30 meters over a course that can vary between 40 and 70 kilometers. He needs to understand the rhythm of the course, reading its turns and climbs for the best moment to change gears, and must know how to make his strength last. For a rider like Indurain, this is easy: He can push a bigger gear, and thus generate more power, longer and harder than anybody else. LeMond was in the same gear as Indurain in a 1992 Tour time trial and still lost four minutes to him.

The ability to suffer the pain of a massive gear is important too. No relaxation is permitted, no unncessary coasting around a curve or down a decline, no yielding to the urge to shift the body or sit up straight for a while and let the back and shoulders relax. His body may be aching, his lungs bursting, his legs weakened from a buildup of lactic acid in his muscles; still he must pedal on. Indurain does this far better than any of the 900 other professional racers. He habitually catches and passes riders who have left two, four and six minutes ahead of him.

Most of his teammates regard him and his strength with what appears to be awe. They also respect the ways of a farmer's son.

"Except for bicycle racing, he has no interests," says Jean-François Bernard, a Frenchman with Banesto. "He's so quiet you don't even hear him. When he comes down to a team meal, you don't even hear him pull his chair away from the table." Other teammates joke that Indurain's hobby is sleeping.

In turn, Indurain regards his teammates and coaches as family. "With Echavarri as the father," he says, "and the other riders as my brothers."

Building a Champion

A former professional racer who rode the 1969 season alongside Anquetil on the BIC team, Echavarri has looked after Indurain for a decade and is one of the three main influences on his professional life.

The first is Eusebio Unzue, who was his directeur sportif with the amateur Reynolds team, one of only three teams Indurain has raced for—CC Villava, his local sports club; Reynolds, a manufacturer of aluminum foil in Navarre, and Banesto, a major Spanish bank. "I met Unzue in 1983," Indurain says. "He taught me how to be realistic: 'Don't run before you can walk,' he always said. With him behind me, I won 14 races in 1984 and he told me it was time to turn professional. That's when I met Echavarri."

When Reynolds decided in 1980 to sponsor a professional team as well as an amateur one, it chose as its directeur sportif Echavarri, who until then ran a bar in Pamplona when he was not coaching the Spanish national amateur team. "I always dreamed about making Miguel a champion," Echavarri says, "but above all I wanted to make him a man. Like Anquetil, who was a fabulous man, whose philosophy was 'Live and let live.' You have to think of yourself but you should never humiliate others. It pleases me very much when people compare Miguel and Anquetil."

Anquetil was legendary for being content—not exuberant—with victory. Asked once how he felt about winning a race by 12 seconds, he replied, "It was 11 more than necessary." Echavarri might have had that attitude in mind when he talked with Philippe Bouvet of the French magazine *Vélo* in the fall of 1992. "Indurain conveys an extraordinary impression of serenity," Bouvet noted, "but does he ever make you worry?" Echavarri replied: "He always impresses me with his intelligence. And with his coolness. In the Giro, there was a stage when all of his rivals attacked at the start while he was taking it easy, letting photographers get pictures of him. The others were already a minute and a half up on him when Indurain said to me, 'Stay calm. There are still 150 kilometers to go.' Obviously I was a lot more nervous than he was."

Indurain remembers how Echavarri guided him, a 20-year-old professional. "He told me, 'You've got time, don't rush, take your time.' I did and I improved every year. And every year he set higher goals for me."

One of the highest was set in 1989, when Echavarri and his pupil attended a gathering of Spanish cycling champions. "I said to him," the directeur sportif remembered, "open your eyes and look at these men. Say to yourself, 'That's me in 20 or 30 years.' And choose whom you want to become."

The third influence, Dr. Francesco Conconi, has helped him choose. Conconi, the Italian who helped Moser set the world record for the hour, has advised Indurain on training schedules and persuaded him, when he weighed 187 pounds early in his professional career, to lose the 10 that allowed him to move into the top rank.

Unzue and Echavarri are with Indurain still on the Banesto team, which, he often says, he never intends to leave. Certainly, he continues, he will not go elsewhere just for money, and nobody doubts his sincerity.

Banesto shielded him well during his two victorious Tours, using Pedro Delgado as a spokesman for Indurain. Delgado also found time to finish sixth overall in 1992. "Having Indurain and Delgado on the same team is like having Goya and Picasso painting for you," Echavarri said.

The two artists, Delgado and Indurain, work well together, especially in a time when the LeMond Doctrine— win the Tour de France and you've won it all—seduces more and more riders. And why not? Victory in the Tour de France confers authority: Palookas can win Paris–Roubaix (Dirk Demol, Jean-Marie Wampers) or even the Vuelta de España (Eric Caritoux, Marco Giovannetti), but who was the last journeyman to win the Tour de France? Therefore that race must be every rider's major goal.

"Oh no," Indurain said early in 1991. "For me, winning the Vuelta is top priority. In the Tour de France, I just ride for Perico," meaning Delgado, the man who had to be protected, even if that kept Indurain from nearly winning the 1990 Tour. He finished 10th overall (to Delgado's fourth) when that race ended with LeMond once again in yellow. Indurain was 12 minutes 47 seconds behind the American—and 11:55 of that was lost in one stage, when team strategy dictated that Indurain serve as Delgado's locomotive over the Madeleine and Glandon Passes to the foot of Alpe d'Huez. By then even a horse like Indurain was winded.

Two days later, on the stage to St. Étienne where LeMond took more than five minutes back from Claudio Chiappucci, Indurain lost 36 more seconds to the American by dropping out of his breakaway to wait for Delgado and pace him in a counterattack. "You know what Spanish journalists call him now?" Delgado joked about his teammate. "St. Miguel the Savior."

No longer. "I was young and I didn't mind that Delgado was the team leader," Indurain said in 1992. "I worked hard for him. When the team asked me to do something for him, I did. That paid off last year. He worked for me." However reluctantly, Indurain began riding the Tour for himself after the first time trial in 1991. He finally admitted, moreover, that the Tour suited him better than the Vuelta. "The pressure is lower away from Spain," he said. "And the weather is better. Coming from the north of Spain, I never like it better than when it's hot, like in the Tour. In the Vuelta, too often it's rainy or cold.

"And the Vuelta isn't my type of race tactically. Too many attacks and surprises. That's Perico's kind of race. In the mountains, he likes to attack, I like to follow." Indurain rarely attacks on a climb.

"What I really like is that the Tour is raced at a higher, faster rhythm than the Vuelta, faster and more continuous. That suits my style."

Having made a strong case for himself in the Tour, Indurain still admitted early in the 1991 season that he would divide team responsibilities with Delgado on familiar lines: the Vuelta for him, the Tour for Perico.

"Indurain was simply too sweet and disciplined a guy to rebel against the team leadership," explained a veteran Spanish journalist. Indurain also seemed to have a bad case of hero worship for Delgado, who had won both the Vuelta and the Tour while Indurain had won neither, finishing second in the Vuelta in 1991. In his own mind, Indurain then appeared to remain the man of the future and Delgado the man of the present.

Indurain put it another way. "The pressure is divided in half and that's good for both of us," he said. Pressure might not have been something Indurain found easy to live with before he began winning the Tour.

Speaking of Echavarri, whom he invariably calls simply Mister, he said, "I trust him entirely. He's directed my career perfectly and given me only good advice. Whatever he asks of me, I'll do it. Whatever is decided is fine with me. I take everything in my stride. I try to keep my emotions under control."

He did not know then that Echavarri had already decided that the future had arrived. "I realized that in 1990," the directeur sportif says, "and it wasn't when Miguel won the stage to Luz Ardiden. It was five days earlier, when he was third in the time trial at Villard de Lans. The day before, he waited for Perico at the Glandon Pass and paced him to the foot of Alpe d'Huez. He was awfully tired in the legs and I didn't know what to expect of him the next day in the time trial.

"And he nearly won it. That day, I said to myself, 'There you are. Miguel is ready.' And he was."

CHAPTER 2

The Challengers

"Revenge?" asked Greg LeMond, repeating a word from a question and rolling it on his tongue like a man sampling a wine. "Revenge? Revenge on whom?" He clearly did not like the taste. "I'm not thinking of revenge, no revenge on anybody. I just want to win the Tour de France again."

In other words, there was nothing personal about his seventh-place finish in the 1991 Tour.

That represented a change for the American rider, who has sometimes taken the race so personally that he feuded with opponents. In 1986, when he won the world's greatest bicycle race for the first time, he quarreled bitterly with Bernard Hinault, his former idol. In 1989, when he won for the second time by nipping Laurent Fignon by eight seconds on the final stage, he and his rival exchanged gibes for months afterward. And in 1990, when he won for the third time, he spent part of the three-week race disparaging the chances of his closest competitor, Claudio Chiappucci.

In 1991, LeMond finished off the first-, second- and third-place victory podium for the first time since his debut in the Tour in 1984. "I've done the Tour six times and been on the podium all but one time—the best record of any rider racing now," he pointed out. "There's no reason why my physical capabilities are diminished from '89 or '90." LeMond was chatting in Fontenay sous Bois, a suburb of Paris, in March 1992 before the start of the Paris–Nice race, which he admitted he had no chance of winning. "No motivation," he explained during an interview in his hotel room. "When I was 24 or 25, I could get motivated for early season races, but not now." He was then a few months shy of his 31st birthday. "Your ability doesn't go down as you get older, but your motivation does. Motivation is like reaching a summit and it's hard to maintain. It's easy to get to the top but hard to stay there."

Was he confident of staying there?

"I have stayed there," he said. "When it comes to the Tour, I have the same motivation I've always had. But for Paris–Nice, it's just part of my training now, part of laying the base for the rest of the season."

The Tour continued to occupy his thoughts, as it has done since he was a teenager in Nevada dreaming about riding in it some day.

"I love the Tour de France," he said with sudden enthusiasm. "I love the world championships, I love Paris–Roubaix. I get excited by those races. I feel like a first-year pro."

Still, when he looked back at 1991, he saw that his best finish in any of those races was his seventh place in the Tour.

"I don't think my seventh place was a disgrace," he said. "There are teams that would kill for a leader who did that well. When you win it, anything but winning is a disappointment though. But not every year can you be at your best."

"There's going to be less pressure on me," LeMond felt. "It's not pressure like you're nervous but the pressure other riders put on you. Everybody is watching and won't let you do anything. Now that I've lost the race, people know I'm beatable. And I'm going to race as if I'm beatable. That means more conservatively."

Another LeMond target for the year was his long-discussed attempt to break the record for the hour's ride against the clock. The standing best time of 51.151 kilometers was set by Francesco Moser of Italy in 1984.

"It all depends on how well I do in the Tour this year," LeMond said, returning to motivation. "If I do well and come out of the Tour fit, we may go for it late in August. But it's definitely secondary to the Tour de France.

"The Tour is still No. 1.

"I'll be 31 years old for the race and I've been a professional for 12 years. Right now I plan to ride just two more years after this season. Time goes by so fast. You realize your career is coming to an end and you want to savor the moments. It's going to be sad being an ex-bike rider coming to the Tour and knowing I'll never ride it again."

Up From the Ranks

Claudio Chiappucci doesn't look, act or sound like somebody who spent much time burning the midnight *olio* when he was a young student in Uboldo, Italy. Mostly *niente*, he says of his academic achievements, admitting that he shone only at recess, when he had a chance to play goalie in soccer. But he must have been paying attention the day his history class discussed Napoleon, another shrimp with humble origins, and his famous dictum: "Every corporal carries a field marshal's baton in his knapsack."

Corporal, at best, was Chiappucci's rank before the 1990 season. After turning professional with Carrera in 1985, he toiled as a domestique as team leaders came and went—Roberto Visentini, Stephen Roche, Urs Zimmermann, Flavio Giupponi. Never did Chiappucci move into their ranks. "I'm an attacker," he likes to boast. "That's my temperament. But I know what people said about me: I make a lot of noise but I don't win." Not until 1989 did he record his first victories, in the Coppa Placci and the Tour of Piedmont.

Then, in 1990, at the age of 27, he exploded: in Paris–Nice, a stage victory and the jersey of the best climber; in the Giro, 12th place and another climber's jersey; in the Tour de France, second place behind Greg LeMond and eight days in the yellow jersey. Coming off the Tour, he finished third in the Championship of Zürich and fourth in two more World Cup races, the Wincanton Classic and the Grand Prix of the Americas. From the depths of the computerized standings of the world's top 900 professionals, Chiappucci vaulted to second place.

Funny, but he didn't sound like a corporal now.

"My goal is to become No. 1 in the next couple of years," he said. He was talking specifically about FICP points but left no doubt that the Tour de France also figured in his ambitions.

"What happened to me last year in the Tour wasn't a piece of luck," he said in 1991. "LeMond was the lucky one, lucky to have a dope like me as his opponent. To tell the truth, LeMond didn't win the Tour—I lost it.

"Let me assure you it would be different now," he warned. When the 78th Tour started in Lyon, he got a chance to prove those words. Although he finished on the victory podium again, in third place this time, he still could not sway those skeptics who did not think of him as a true champion.

Among those was LeMond. "It's one thing to have a good Tour de France, it's another to win the Tour de France," he noted. "There's a big difference between third and first." Or even second and first. Chiappucci, he gets no respect.

He was a grand part of the Italian Renaissance in cycling— victories by riders from the Boot in six classics and two major tours in 1990—but still people tended to write him off. Other Italian stars, mainly Gianni Bugno and Moreno Argentin, made no secret of their dislike for him and his strong ambitions. He was not always respected on his Carerra team. "When you get a puncture, he doesn't always listen when you holler at him to tow you back to the pack," a teammate complained while Chiappucci was still a domestique.

This animosity filtered through to the *tifosi*, the overheated Italian fans, whose hearts belonged to Bugno. Chiappucci might have finished second in the 1990 Tour and Bugno seventh, the *tifosi* said, but it was Bugno who recorded victories in the two most prestigious stages, the fabled climb at Alpe d'Huez and the sprinter's showcase at Bordeaux.

Basta, Chiappucci decided, enough. "I rode for 143 days last year, more than any other rider," he said. "The same for the two years before that." He was so busy working to better himself, he added, that once again he had been unable to find time in the off-season to marry his fiancée,

Rita. (Until his long-delayed marriage late in 1992, Chiappucci lived with his mother, a redoubtable type who traveled to Lourdes when the Tour stopped there in 1990 and made a well-publicized visit to the grotto to pray, vainly, for his success.)

In the spring of 1991, a new Chiappucci showed up after another winter spent riding cyclocross when he wasn't attending testimonial dinners at every school, orphanage and old folks' home in his native province of Lombardy. "Anybody who invited me, I showed up," he reported.

The corporal had grasped the baton.

He started getting star treatment from his Carrera directeur sportif, the savvy Davide Bofiva. Suddenly Chiappucci was a franchise rider, the right man in the right place, as Carrera, after years of glory, was no longer deep in Italian riders capable of winning races. Del Tongo had Franco Ballerini and Mario Cipollini, Ariostea had Argentin and Adriano Baffi, Gatorade had Bugno and Marco Giovannetti. Behind Chiappucci, Carrera had only an aging Guido Bontempi.

Reveling in their depth and newfound ambition, major Italian teams had ended years of isolation and begun competing seriously outside the home country. The Tour de France, not the Giro, became Bugno's prime goal as he—and Chiappucci, of course—hoped to become the first Italian to win it since Felice Gimondi in 1965. In this new international atmosphere, Carrera decided to let Chiappucci skip the traditional early races at home and go instead to Spain. While the rest of his compatriots were riding Tirreno–Adriatico to prepare for Milan–San Remo, the first World Cup classic and the showpiece of the early Italian season, he was finishing second in the Tour of Murcia and fourth in the Catalan Week, where he pulled off a rare double by winning a mass sprint in the morning and a time trial in the afternoon. That done, he returned the next night to Italy.

Chiappucci made his move halfway along the 294-kilo-meter Milan–San Remo, attacking at the exit of the Turchino mountain tunnel and speeding away on the descent. Chiappucci cruised into San Remo a winner by 45 seconds. "Any time I can attack and make people suffer, I'm off," Chiappucci said while he waited for the pack to show up.

Third in the 1991 Tour de France, second in the 1992 Giro: The FICP points were pouring in and, as Bugno languished through a dreary spring, the gap between them began to close substantially. Suddenly the No. 1 ranking did not seem such an outlandish goal for Chiappucci, the little corporal no more.

Too Much Pressure

The United States is a huge country and Gianni Bugno hoped to lose himself there, just another face in the crowd, for 10 days during the spring of 1992. Back home in Italy, he said, there's too much pressure.

At age 28 and the peak of his art, Bugno should have been a happy man. He ranked first then among the world's professional bicycle racers and he wore the rainbow-striped jersey of the world champion on the road. But, while he may have been first in war and first in peace, he was last in the hearts of his countrymen.

"No, no," Bugno protested. "Not the fans, it's the press. The fans understand. The newspapers put all this pressure on me."

There was no question that Bugno was a champion but he was not yet the champion he would like to be. For that, he would have to win the Tour de France.

"The Tour de France is the biggest race there is, the most beautiful, the most important," Bugno said. "When you've won the Tour de France, you've won it all." Bugno had come close to winning it, having finished seventh in his debut in 1990 and second in 1991. For 1992 he focused his program on nothing but the Tour and decided that the demanding Giro would reduce his chances in the French race in July. Less long and less challenging, the Tour Du Pont in the United States in May fit right into his schedule. Plus it was wonderfully distant from home: *La Gazzetta dello Sport* was the only Italian paper that sent a reporter to the Du Pont.

Bugno had nice things to say about the Tour Du Pont, which was in its second year as a successor to the Tour de Trump and which bills itself accurately as "America's premier cycling event." Attracting 15 teams of 7 riders each, the Du Pont covered 1,000 miles in Delaware, Pennsylvania, Maryland and Virginia before ending in Washington, D.C.

"It's not a training race for us," Bugno said. "It's a good race and we're here to do the maximum, myself and the team. A good showing here would boost our morale before the Giro."

The Giro: There was that word again.

Bugno won the Giro in 1990 when he emerged as the star of the Italian Renaissance in bicycle racing. Until 1990 he was a somewhat humble rider, content enough to win minor races in Piedmont and the Apennines, but a secret sufferer from vertigo or dizziness and fear of falling. The problem was laid to a bad crash in the 1988 Giro and to a congenital obstruction in the canals of his inner ear. As a cure, Bugno tried ultrasound treatments laced with music, mostly Mozart.

"I listened to Mozart at different speeds and degrees of loudness for a month," he said. "After that, the vertigo was gone." Next he visited an allergist, who discovered that he could not tolerate wheat, milk and milk products. Pills were prescribed and his diet was changed.

Then came counseling by a psychologist, who helped resolve Bugno's timidity. The problem was traced to his childhood, which he spent with his grandparents in Italy while his parents worked in Switzerland, where Bugno was born.

By 1990 Bugno was a champion and now his ambitions were soaring to the greatest race of them all. Now he thought of nothing less than becoming the first Italian to win the Tour de France in 30 years.

"Twenty-seven years," he said in correction. Bugno knew very well that Felice Gimondi was the last Italian to win the Tour, in 1965.

The major obstacle, he admitted, was Miguel Indurain. "Last year Indurain was very, very strong," the Italian said. "I hardly made any mistakes but he was just too strong. I did my best but he was too strong.

"Indurain, LeMond, many others—they all want to win too but only one rider gets to finish first," Bugno said. "Win or not, as long as I do my best, I'll be satisfied."

Really? Did his second place in the 1991 Tour satisfy him as much as his victory in the Giro d'Italia?

"No," Bugno replied. "It's always better to win, of course. Second, it's not much."

CHAPTER 3

Going for Four

Hours before the 1991 Tour de France began in Lyon, something was wrong with Greg LeMond, some spark was missing. A person who usually radiates confidence in his athletic talent, LeMond sounded uncharacteristically tentative.

"I'm nervous," he admitted before he sought his third successive victory in the race and fourth overall. Partly behind that nervousness, he said in a frank interview, was a profound disappointment in his lack of victories and a weariness with continuing criticism of his performances.

More important, he continued, was his realization that his physical condition was not what it should be and that there seemed to be nothing immediate he could do to improve. Longer range—over the Tour's first 10 days of racing on flat territory—he remained hopeful.

"I don't feel I'm at my very best right now," LeMond said as he was being driven through the backstreets of Lyon to a news conference. "I hope I do improve between here and the Pyrenees and Alps. An athlete's not programmable. I can't be programmed to be at my very best for the Tour. I've done a lot of work this year and things haven't come together as I hoped."

The result was his belief that 1991 might not be his year to win the Tour de France. In five previous appearances, he finished third in 1984, second in 1985 and first in 1986, '89 and '90. He missed the 1987 race after he was nearly killed in a hunting accident and the '88 race because of tendon problems.

"I am aware that one day I'm going to be beat in the Tour," LeMond said slowly. "I hope it's not this year, but it could be. A lot of good riders are coming on strong and that's going to make it a tough Tour."

Then he brightened, as if he were shocked by his own words. A rider who never predicts victory, LeMond rarely foresees defeat, and never before in a race as dear to him as the Tour de France.

"I felt the same way last year—everybody coming on so strong," he continued. "So there's really not much difference.

"I always feel this way," he insisted in a claim open to challenge. "But last year I felt I was really good at the Tour of Switzerland. I had that confidence coming into the Tour de France.

"This year..." he said as his voice trailed away.

LeMond finished his warmup for the Tour, the Tour of Switzerland, in 22d place and admitted that he rode well only a few days. He blamed the weather, which was mainly overcast or rainy in Europe most of the spring. "I'm a warm weather racer and this heat feels good," he said in summery Lyon as he slipped into the car and cranked open the sun roof.

Before the Tour of Switzerland, again in cold and rainy weather, he dropped out of the Giro d'Italia when he was far behind and some of the hardest climbing was still to come. Those two results, coupled with the fact that he had not won a race since the last Tour de France, left him wondering exactly what he could expect of his body and his fabled ability to recover overnight from the rigors of each stage in the three-week Tour.

"I'd prefer to have a good test already before me—a good place in the Tour of Switzerland, a good place in the Tour of Italy," he said. "I think I'm O.K. I just don't know. I can't even tell you. I don't know."

Melded into this uncertainty was LeMond's awareness that a handful of his opponents appeared to be at top form.

"I just wasn't in very good shape," LeMond said of his appearance in the Giro, which was dominated by Italian riders. "I was in decent shape but these guys were in very good shape. These guys were like me usually in the Tour de France. Year after year, people just seem to be getting in a little bit better shape and that makes a big difference if you're not following that same level."

He left no doubt that he was not at that level for the start of the Tour, either physically or mentally.

"My head follows my physical condition," he said. "If I feel good, there's no problem with my motivation and determination. But if I'm a little..." Again his words trailed off.

Suddenly, as his car neared the Tour's headquarters, where LeMond was to hold a press conference, he exploded.

"I'm nervous," he said angrily. "I'm tired of talking about the same questions every time: What do you think about the critics, Merckx, this and that, Moser. It just gets old, you know. The same questions. Every year it's the same."

Eddy Merckx and Francesco Moser had been outspoken all season in denouncing what they interpreted as LeMond's attitude and his lack of victories, including no individual stages in the 1990 Tour.

"I want to win the Tour," LeMond continued. "If a stage victory comes along, I'm going to nab it. But I'm tired of people talking about I didn't win stage victories. I didn't win stages last year but I won the Tour de France."

That reminder ended his rage.

"I wasn't certain I was going to be great last year but I did have a little bit better physical feeling the week before the Tour," he said calmly. "But this doesn't mean," and here he broke into a laugh, "that I'm already defeated. I just think I might have not a great start of the Tour and I could work myself into it.

"The Tour de France I look at as a three-week race. Even if you do have a bad day, there's a possibility to take it back. The race isn't over until you hit the Champs-Élysées. In the Tour de France, there's only one thing that tells the truth and that's the winner at the end."

Turning the Heat Up

Maybe Greg LeMond was right when he said that all he needed to turn his year around was some hot weather. Finding temperatures in the 80s and 90s in Lyon for the start of the Tour, LeMond finished part of his first weekend's work in a familiar garment, the yellow jersey.

He won it—and later lost it—the hard way. After finishing third in the prologue behind Thierry Marie of Castorama and Erik Breukink of PDM, he helped drive a breakaway by 11 riders during the first of two half-day stages. Eight of the 11 gained one minute 44 seconds over the rest of the 198-man field.

In the second stage of the day, a team time trial over 36.5 kilometers, LeMond was slowed by a flat and lost enough seconds that he fell back to second place overall. The new leader was Rolf Sörensen, a Dane with Ariostea, who was no threat in the long run because he is a weak climber.

A far bigger loser in the team time trial was Stephen Roche, the Irishman who won the Tour in 1987. Troubled by cramps, Roche said he had been in the toilet, thinking he had 15 minutes to spare, when his Tonton Tapis went to the starting line. Although they tried to stall, the riders had to leave without Roche. The Irishman set off seven minutes behind the team, rode alone and finished 14 minutes 20 seconds behind, far outside the permitted time differential of 11 minutes. Despite his protests, Roche was eliminated.

After his bicycle flatted in the time trial, LeMond pushed his Z team to make up the time, taking frequent pulls at the front. Ariostea was too fast, however, and Sörensen had trailed by only 23 seconds. He now led by 33.

"We missed a very good break," said Steve Bauer, a Canadian with the Motorola team. "It's a significant one." Bauer was an authority on significant breakaways in the

Tour, of course, after the one in 1990 that gave him the yellow jersey.

"It's not as much time as last year but it's more meaningful because there are better riders than last year in front now," judged Phil Anderson, an Australian with Motorola.

Among those leaders were some of LeMond's companions in the breakaway. They included notably Breukink, who finished third in the previous Tour, and his teammate Raul Alcala, a Mexican who finished eighth in 1990. Breukink now ranked third overall.

The 114.5-kilometer morning stage was won by Djamolidine Abdoujaparov, an Uzbek with Carrera and the strongest Soviet finisher since Stalin. Sean Kelly, an Irishman with PDM, was just behind in the sprint finish by 8 of the 11 riders. Third was LeMond, who thus added four bonus seconds to the 10 he had collected by finishing first and second in two bonus sprints along the way.

The morning stage passed through the graceless urban conglomeration surrounding Lyon, France's second city—not much of a distinction in a country where the telephone code is No. 1 for Paris and No. 16 for everywhere else.

Racing over narrow, snaky and rolling roads, the field of 9 riders on each of 22 teams had to wait only five kilometers for the first attack: Rolf Jaermann, a Swiss with Weinmann, went off alone and stayed there over the only two elevations of the day, earning himself the mountain climber's jersey.

After 45 kilometers of solitude, he was joined by the 10 others.

"The pack was very nervous right from the start and I told myself to seize any opportunity," LeMond said later. "Alcala was one of the first to go and I wasn't about to let him go alone. Then we all cooperated in the break."

The Long Road Home

Every Tour de France should have at least one happy story, and here it is:

The next time somebody attempts to justify a dirty deed by announcing that life isn't fair, Ronan Pensec intends to set him straight. "Life, she's fair," he said, practicing his English. "She's more than fair."

Pensec knows, even though he can look back on a childhood marked by the death of his mother when he was 7 and of his father 10 years later.

"I learned young to live life," he says. To pay his bills, he became a bicycle racer in his native Brittany and was successful enough to turn professional at age 21. His results have been respectable, including a sixth place in the 1986 Tour de France and an eighth place in the '88 Tour. He missed the 1987 Tour after he injured a heel and spent that July bemoaning his bad luck.

"For a bicycle rider to miss the Tour de France is bad," he feels. "But for a French bicycle rider to miss the Tour, it's a calamity. A tragedy. Worse."

Pensec spoke those words during the 1991 Tour Du Pont, and his tone was portentous. At that point he faced the very real possibility that he would miss the Tour de France.

The problem was eligibility. His new team, Seur, did not rank high enough to gain an automatic invitation and was hoping to qualify as one of six wildcards. Seur's chances were slim, unlike those of Pensec's former team, Z. Now it was led by Greg LeMond but, before he was hired, Pensec was Z's main rider.

In the 1990 Tour, Pensec was one of the four riders who broke away on the first stage and established a 10-minute lead. Fourth overall, he attacked on the first day in the mountains more than a week later and took over the yellow jersey.

That lasted only two days, as the pressure and the travail of climbing got to him. He eventually finished the Tour in 20th place but first won a special place in the hearts of his fellow Frenchmen. What endeared him to them was Pensec's sweetness. Despite his punk style and spikey hairdo, he is really a sheep in wolf's clothing. Face to face, his manner is reasonable and polite.

At the end of the season, Pensec announced that although he was happy riding for LeMond, he planned to join Seur in Spain. He would more than double his salary to $400,000 a year and become a team leader again, but those were not the only reasons he was leaving.

He wanted to see more of the world, he explained during the Du Pont. He knew France well and the United States a bit from races and vacations there, working on his English and shopping for motorcycles with his friend Bob Roll of the Motorola team. Now it was time to live in another country, far from his home in Quimper in Brittany.

There's a whole world out there, Pensec said, and he wanted to become a citizen of it. Who knows? he asked, maybe he would ride for an Italian team next.

These hopes began turning sour when it grew increasingly doubtful that Seur would be asked to ride in the Tour de France. Not helping was the fact that Pensec had a bad spring, missing 18 days with assorted ailments, including a deeply sprained left wrist that he wore in a bandage during the Du Pont.

The bad news came in mid-June: Seur had not made the list but was the first alternate.

"I heard that the Tonton Tapis team, which was invited, might not accept," he said. "So I called to check, but they said they would accept. Everybody else was certain."

"It broke my heart," he continued. "To hear that I would not be in the Tour was really hard on me, dramatic."

Adding to the heartbreak was his knowledge that the Tour would finish a stage in his hometown of Quimper on July 15 and start there the next day.

He wanted so much to be part of the race in front of his neighbors and all the others in the city of 50,000 who knew him. "It would mean so much to me and my wife Armelle," he said.

Late in June Pensec raced well in Spain and then finished a good 14th in the French national championships. He began making plans to spend Tour de France time in some of the minor races that dot the calendar in other countries.

Five days before the start of the Tour, however, he was asked to be in Madrid. Representatives of the Amaya team, which had accepted an invitation to the Tour de France, wanted to meet with him and officials of the Seur team. Amaya's goal was to buy his contract.

"Oh, I was very, very happy when I heard about this," Pensec said. "The Tour de France is my life and the stage is in my town."

Signing a rider from another team in mid-season is rare but not unknown, and the deal was done quickly. Everybody was happy—Amaya got a rider it wanted, Seur was relieved of a big salary during a time of small races and Pensec made it to the Tour.

The deal began to look even better for everybody at the end of the first week, when Amaya's leader, Fabio Parra, broke two ribs in a crash and had to withdraw from the Tour. Pensec was promoted to the main role.

Even before that, he was thrilled with his newfound chance. "A lot of people were happy, me most," he said of his signing. "I get to ride in the Tour de France after all and go to Quimper."

Quimper is a city known for its shellfish and painted pottery. Quimper has many charms. Mainly, for Ronan Pensec, citizen of the world, it's home.

Sprinters to the Fore

Stage by stage, the Tour rolled counterclockwise around France toward its first major rendezvous, the 73-kilometer individual time trial scheduled as the eighth stage from Argentan to Alencon. The sprinters battled it out, with Étienne de Wilde of Histor, Djamolidine Abdoujaparov of Carrera and Jelle Nijdam of Buckler victorious on consecutive days and Rolf Sörensen easily retaining the yellow jersey until, on the fifth stage, the Dane crashed and fractured his left shoulderblade. Courageously, he got back on a teammate's bicycle and finished the last four kilometers but that night he announced that he could not continue. Although a yellow jersey was sent to Greg LeMond at his hotel, the American elegantly said that, out of respect for Sörensen, he would not wear it the next morning. When the sixth stage began, therefore, the Tour de France was in the rare position of not having anybody in the maillot jaune.

Not for long, though, Thierry Marie of Castorama, the winner of the prologue, kept a promise he had made the previous fall, when the route of the 1991 Tour was announced. Seeing that the race would pass through his native Normandy, Marie told the president of his first club, Livarot, that he would come home in the yellow jersey.

At kilometer 25 of the 259-kilometer stage from Arras to Le Havre, Marie attacked alone. He was not seen again by the pack. Before he was done, Marie had built a lead of nearly 20 minutes, which was whittled down to 1 minute 54 seconds at the finish, enough to put Marie into the race's lead by nearly a minute. The next stage was again a sprint finish, won this time by Jean-Paul van Poppel of PDM, and then it was the day of the first real shootout.

Growing stronger as the 45-mile time trial course grew longer, LeMond stormed back into the lead of the Tour and opened up more breathing room between himself and most of his challengers. He also answered most affirmatively a question he had asked.

"Before the Tour started, I said I'd wait a week for this stage before I could say how my form was," he said after he finished. "Now I've got the answer." And that answer was that he seemed fine.

For all that, LeMond finished second in the stage, eight seconds behind Miguel Indurain. The Spaniard's teammate Jean-François Bernard, a Frenchman, was third, 53 seconds behind Indurain and 45 behind LeMond. Then began the long roll-call of challengers to the defending champion. Fourth was Erik Breukink, who lost 1:06 to the American. In itself, that was not a heavy defeat but Breukink had been favored in the time trial. He is a specialist in the exercise and won the Tour Du Pont by easily triumphing in a time trial on the final day.

By the end of the overcast and windy afternoon, LeMond was back in the yellow jersey and looking pleased. He now had a lead of 1:13 on Breukink and 2:17 on Indurain, with all the other challengers at least four minutes behind.

"You can't refuse the yellow jersey," LeMond said when he was asked if he would defend it at all costs in the next three days over flat terrain. "But my goal is to win the Tour de France. For that, you have to race intelligently and not let your ego decide your tactics."

Tens of thousands of fans lined the long and rolling course in Normandy, lured by the sight of a native son, Marie, in the yellow jersey. But his long solo breakaway two days earlier obviously left him exhausted and he finished the time trial in 35th place and fell back to eighth overall.

Since the race was run in inverse order of standing, Marie was the last to start. Setting off ahead of him, two minutes apart, were Breukink, in fifth place and LeMond, in fourth.

The American said beforehand that he would be happy to limit his loss to the Dutchman to 30 seconds and that was almost exactly the time he trailed with about 13 miles to go. Down by 26 seconds then, LeMond said later that "I just went flat out right to the end." In the same distance, Breukink grew tired and began to lose speed. "Suddenly my legs felt heavy, very heavy," he reported. His smooth stroke turned choppy and he began thrusting with his upper body, which is usually as immobile as a bust on a pedestal.

LeMond rides in a different style, looking more like a swimmer as he hunches over his extended handlebars and occasionally puts his head up, as if gulping for air. It is not as classic as Breukink's style and sometimes not as efficient—in the Du Pont time trial, LeMond was second to the Dutchman by 35 seconds. But this was a different race.

"The Tour transforms me," LeMond told interviewers, who could not quarrel with him. At that point only Breukink and Indurain seemed to remain as major challengers and the Spaniard, the best climber of the three, sounded uncertain.

Asked if he thought he could win this Tour de France, Indurain hedged. "I want to win the Tour some day," he said. "Maybe this year, maybe next." He did not sound at all confident.

Mystery Ailment

Traveling through Normandy and Brittany on the flat, the favorites remained hidden in the pack and left sprint finishes to Mauro Ribeiro of RMO, who became the first Brazilian to win a Tour stage, followed by Phil Anderson of Motorola. The Australian was enjoying a remarkable comeback year but his victory at Quimper was upstaged when the PDM team withdrew from the Tour, blaming a mysterious ailment that team officials said they suspected was food poisoning. The casualties included Erik Breukink, who was third in the overall standings.

Five riders for PDM, ranked No. 1 in the professional world, dropped out during the stage and the remaining four were not allowed by their directeur sportif, Jan Gisbers, to start the next morning because they were afflicted with high temperatures and pain.

"Erik says he has a fever and hurts very much in his head and body," reported Breukink's wife, Gea, from their home in Kalmthout, Belgium. "Not in his stomach, though. He says his stomach is fine."

None of the more than half dozen non-riders who accompanied the team was affected.

At first Tour doctors suspected a viral ailment and discounted the possibility of food poisoning. Managers of the last three hotels the team had stopped at pointed out that PDM officials, mechanics and masseurs had eaten the same food as the riders and that none of them had fallen ill.

In St. Herblain, the town in Brittany where the 11th stage ended, a PDM spokesman, Jonathan Boyer, said that tests carried out in a Dutch hospital on Nico Verhoeven, the first rider to pull out, hinted at a bacteriological infection. "The tests showed 95 percent probability that it was linked to food or to drink," Boyer said. "It is certainly not a viral problem. The riders were taken ill over Sunday night but we don't know what it was that got them."

Gisbers was equally insistent. "There are two specialists in the Netherlands and they're nearly 100 percent sure it's bacteria and are nearly 100 percent sure that it had something to do with some food poisoning," he said.

In Rennes, where the team stayed at the Hotel du Cheval d'Or after the ninth stage, a spokesman, Valérie Rossi, strongly denied that the riders had gotten sick there. "They ate what everybody ate," she said. On the dinner menu were quiche Lorraine, vegetable soup, grilled chicken, spaghetti, mashed potatoes, zucchini and yoghurt. "Besides," she added, "when they got here, one of them was already sick." That was Verhoeven, who had a temperature of 40°C (104° Fahrenheit) then. It had since dropped to 38 degrees (100.5) and he had been discharged from the hospital in Den Bosch, Boyer said.

The two nights before, after the time trial, the team stayed at the Hotel St. Pierre in Rancs, where the menu included grilled chicken both nights. Rice and spaghetti accompanied it. "There was no complaint about the food and nobody who ate with them became sick," said the owner, Mrs. Françoise Delaunay.

The withdrawal of the team for medical reasons was described as a first in the history of the Tour de France.

The first five riders to drop out were Verhoeven, Jean-Paul van Poppel, Uwe Raab, Falk Boden and Martin Earley. The second group comprised Breukink, Raul Alcala, Jos Van Aert and Sean Kelly.

If Anderson's glory after his victory at Quimper had been fleeting, the winner of the next stage was nearly unnoticed in the sensation surrounding PDM's withdrawal. Once again, Charly Mottet, a Frenchman with the RMO team, barely struggled into the headlines despite his victory.

Yet Another Explanation

The shadow of the syringe had fallen across professional bicycle racing.

It followed revelations, months after the Tour ended, that a doctor for the PDM team had injected all nine riders with liquid food before they were forced to quit the race with body pains and high fevers. The injections were legal but never made public as a possible cause of the withdrawals or as part of the team's routine medical treatment.

The organizers of the Tour accepted findings that the liquid food was probably contaminated.

A viral infection was first suspected but PDM's management insisted that food poisoning was the problem. Months later, in a team study that was made public, strong suspicion fell on injections of Intralipid, an over-the-counter food supplement containing lecithin, a derivative of egg yolk, and soybean oil.

The use of hypodermic needles summoned up dramatic connotations in the popular mind, officials and observers of the sport admitted ruefully. "If it comes out of a syringe, the public thinks it probably has to be dope," said David Walsh, an Irish journalist and the biographer of his country's two leading riders, Stephen Roche and Sean Kelly.

"You're not dealing with a doping scandal here," insisted a PDM rider who spoke only on condition of anonymity. "What happened was defensible.

"But," he admitted, "something went wrong somewhere."

He, Walsh and others were quick to deny that there was anything sinister in the common, if unpublicized, practice of injections. "Whatever it looks like," Walsh said, "many teams prefer injections to pills or syrup because injections work faster."

That was supported by the directeur sportif of a professional team, who also insisted on anonymity. "Too many pills upset the stomach," he said. "So one injection is better than 20 pills.

"Of course," he added, "nobody needs to take 20 pills either.

"With injections, however, there's a psychological advantage for some riders. It hurts, so they can think they're getting something that the other riders don't have. Many traditional teams create a feeling with their riders that if they don't have injections, they feel less confident."

Another directeur sportif, Jan Raas of Buckler, confirmed that injections were not uncommon. "But not food supplements with us, no, no, no, no," he said. "Some vitamin injections, sometimes glucose but not more than that."

Injections by riders themselves without benefit of medical advice was standard when Raas was in his heyday as a rider a decade ago. He won 10 stages in the Tour de France and was world road-race champion in 1978.

"In my time there were no team doctors," he said. "Doctors are better because you can trust them." Medical practice was often dispensed then by soigneurs—mechanics or masseurs.

"I never did injections myself because I was a little bit afraid of them, always," Raas continued. "I took vitamin pills and iron pills."

Do some riders still inject themselves? "It's a good question," he responded. "I don't know."

At a news conference near the end of the Tour, PDM officials strongly denied that drugs had been involved. The French press and television made such suggestions immediately after the withdrawals, talking openly about doping or blood packing gone wrong.

"We reject any insinuations about drugs," said Manfred Krikke, the manager of the PDM team. He and PDM's medical authorities said that salmonella was the prime suspect. "There is absolutely no drug use involved," added

Professor Jacques van Rossum of the department of pharmacology at the University of Nijmegen in the Netherlands.

Since no PDM riders failed any of the four drug tests administered to them, the Tour's doctors did no further investigating, leaving the affair to the team.

In a telephone conversation from the Netherlands after the PDM announcement, Krikke offered two possible reasons for the contamination. One was that the food supplement, which was injected three times during the race, had been stored in high heat in a car. The other was that the needle used might have contained air, which he described as "good growing ground for bacteria."

He described the supplement as "standard food in hospitals, used for patients who have stomach problems or are in a coma." Its use had been discontinued by PDM, he added.

Jan Gisbers, the team's directeur sportif, explained that the use of food supplements in forms other than injections had been standard practice for the last half dozen years at least.

"You have to do it," he said, "because of the calories a rider burns. In a heavy racing day, he needs more than 6,000 calories, sometimes 9,000 to 10,000." Professional riders eat big breakfasts, usually based on carbohydrates, and big dinners, usually based on proteins. During a daily stage they consume one or two lunches, which are eaten on the fly from canvas bags packed with small sandwiches, pastries and fruit.

The average rider will also drink up to a dozen bottles of liquid during a race, mainly water but increasingly high-energy compounds.

Gisbers added that not all nine riders had received three injections in their arms during the Tour. "Some got two shots, some three," he said. "But the last time, they all received it." That was at Rennes, a day before the first rider fell sick.

Into the Pyrenees

The Tour shattered on several planes the next day as Greg LeMond lost his yellow jersey, the leadership of the race was rearranged and the riders staged a 40-minute strike and broke international rules by not wearing rigid helmets. Almost as a footnote, the Tour's organizers permitted a disqualified rider to compete and said they would decide afterward whether to recognize his performance. (They did.)

That was for openers.

The closer was a three-man finish more than seven minutes ahead of the former leadership. Luc Leblanc, a Frenchman with the Castorama team, vaulted from that finish into the yellow jersey.

"I don't believe it," he said, and he was not alone. A promising rider for the last three years, Leblanc at age 24 had never won a major race and not many minor ones either. The 192-kilometer 12th stage on the first day in the Pyrenees was won by Charly Mottet, who recorded his second consecutive stage victory in the Tour and once again was shouldered off center stage.

Second, by a shade, was Pascal Richard, a Swiss with Helvetia. Knowing that he was now the new race leader, Leblanc courteously disdained to fight it out with them in the sprint and finished two seconds back in third place.

Two minutes 6 seconds behind the winner were Andy Hampsten, an American with Motorola, and Maurizio Fondriest, an Italian with Panasonic. Everybody else was at least four minutes slower. So, at the end of a gloriously hot, sunny and clear day, Leblanc had moved from sixth place into first, 2:35 ahead of LeMond, in second place, and 3:52 ahead of Mottet in third.

How meaningful the shake-up was remained a matter of dispute. Leblanc had no reputation as a consistently strong climber and might be expected to fall apart as early as the next day, when the really big mountains in the Pyrenees were to be attacked. On the other hand, as they say, he might do well there too. The yellow jersey has a way of transforming a talented young rider.

Mottet was another puzzle. At age 28, he had been a pre-Tour favorite for many years but always wilted under the pressure. Although he proclaimed that he would not ride for overall victory but would concentrate on daily triumphs, his continuing success and his third place might have lit a spark in some recessed part of his spirit.

All in all, it was an action-packed day, including even a race.

After its 40-minute refusal to start, the pack rode swiftly through routinely beautiful low country of vineyards and fields full of corn, sheep and sleek silver cattle. On the first major climb, the 1,540-meter-high Soudet, riders began to attack, splintering the field, now down to 185 men.

Leblanc, Richard, Hampsten and Fondriest were among the five riders who thrust ahead and built a five-minute lead as they passed the summit. Mottet joined them soon afterward and they pulled together up and down the next two climbs to pad their lead.

On the final 30-kilometer descent from France into Spain, Leblanc attacked the group and was answered only by Mottet and Richard. "We collaborated perfectly," the new yellow jersey reported with a huge smile.

Another big beamer at the finish was Urs Zimmermann, a Swiss with the Motorola team, who was put out of the race late the night before and then allowed to compete while a final decision on his status was being mulled over.

Zimmermann's offense was that, on the race's day off, he did not take the assigned plane from Brittany to the start in Pau, France. He traveled the 580 kilometers instead by team car.

"I was afraid to go by plane," Zimmermann said in the morning as he sat hunched and dark-eyed in a team car at the start. "I had this feeling that we would crash and I couldn't face the flight. So I came by car. I've been afraid before but always the flight was so long that it would have been impossible to take a car. Here it was reasonable to take the car."

His change in plans violated a new and little-known Tour rule against independent travel and resulted in his expulsion. Another rider who traveled on his own, the third-place finisher Richard, brought a doctor's note and was let off with a warning.

Both riders' directeurs sportifs, however, were banned for the day.

"It's not like we were trying to cheat," argued Zimmermann's teammate, Ron Kiefel. "There's no gain in this. We just didn't know the rule. It doesn't make any sense that a guy fails a drug test and gets a 10-minute penalty and Zimmy takes a car and is out of the race."

Zimmermann's cause was adopted by all of his fellow riders, who refused to begin while demanding that he be reinstated and that they all not have to wear helmets on the sweltering climbs. Rigid shell helmets were made compulsory in 1991 but ribbed helmets had been allowed as a compromise.

Finally, to get the proceedings under way, Zimmermann, who had been waiting in full uniform, was allowed to bolt from the car and mount his bicycle. "I don't know how I'll do because the pressure has been terrible," he said.

Although he was involved in the first big break, he finished far back.

As for the helmets, most riders went without them and faced fines of 300 Swiss francs (about $250) each. Under the rules, any rider showing up bareheaded could have been expelled from the race, like Zimmermann.

A Bunch of Hotheads

Despite abundant anecdotal evidence to the contrary, there are no blockheads out there: At its thickest, the human skull measures no more than four tenths of an inch. At its thinnest, it measures considerably less.

The average highway, on the other hand, measures two to three inches of tar, concrete or asphalt laid over a hardened roadbed many times deeper. In any sharp and sudden meeting of skull and highway, the highway always prevails.

This truth causes about 800 bicycling deaths in the United States each year (serious but nonfatal injuries suffered while cycling account for 10 times that total annually.) Even at the highest level of the sport, the professional world, a death or disabling injury was recorded nearly every year in the last decade.

These statistics led to a ruling that, beginning with the 1991 season, rigid helmets had be worn by all riders in races sanctioned by the International Cycling Union, which governs amateur and professional competition and is known as the UCI after its initials in French. The rule followed by a couple of years a mandate that helmets must be worn in all races in the United States. At the heart of the rule was a 1988 report in the respected New England Journal of Medicine that helmets could reduce the risk of head injury by 85 percent and the risk of brain injury by 88 percent.

Professional riders reacted to the imposition of mandatory helmets with a rare vehemence. Never, they said, had a rule been so worthy and so unfair. Complaints ranged from the extra heat that helmets generate on a summer's climb, to the perceived autocratic manner in which the rule was imposed, to the Darth Vader stormtrooper look produced when helmets are combined with the riders' omnipresent sunglasses.

The rule was so controversial in the European professional pack, in fact, that the riders succeeded in getting it reversed. All it took was a mass boycott of helmets at two early races and a threat to disrupt the World Cup round of classics. The reversal allowed all parties to save face, with the riders acknowledging in a statement that helmets improve safety and the UCI saying that the next move was up to helmet manufacturers to produce a cooler model.

"We're convinced that helmet manufacturers can come up with a solution," said Hein Verbruggen, then president of the International Federation of Professional Cycling, which is known as the FICP. That sort of diplomacy led later in the year to his promotion to head of the UCI.

Even before the turnaround, manufacturers themselves seemed less sure that they could solve the problem.

"Climbing that hill at Alpe d'Huez is never fun and there's no way to make it fun," said Jim Gentes, the founder of Giro Helmets in California. "But we're not talking discomfort here, we're talking protection.

"Let's face it: Bike racing is a very dangerous sport. Riders die of head injuries. I'm amazed how many times people land on their heads.

"We all have the attitude that it can't happen and then all of a sudden somebody dies." He cited the case of Joaquim Agostinho, a leading Tour de France rider who was killed in his native Portugal after a heavy fall in the Tour of the Algarve in 1984.

At that time, a year before the development of the hardshell helmet, professionals occasionally wore the striped leather helmets known as "hairnets."

"Hairnets offer minimum protection because they have no shock absorption," explained Charles Luthi, the managing director of Bell Helmets Europe. "They were better than nothing, but not by much."

Luthi agreed that a helmet would make a mountain stage in the Tour de France hotter. "I've seen riders try to tear off their clothes in that heat. So, of course, the helmet and its chinstrap will add to the discomfort. The trick is to get the right helmet, one that allows maximum ventilation while providing maximum protection."

After the UCI reversal, Luthi sounded both worried and relieved.

"It looks like they're killing the rule forever," he said, "because how do you measure comfort? You'll never get all the riders to agree on that. This is too bad because they're confusing security with comfort."

That was the worrisome part. The relief followed quickly.

"I'm not unhappy with the reversal," Luthi said. "This controversy could have gone on all season and then helmets would have become really unpopular, especially with young riders. This way it's over and we can continue to try to get young riders into helmets and save some lives."

As Luthi noted, security and comfort were confused in the helmet war. When tempers were at their peak, the riders were strongly denounced by Verbruggen. "For me, they're acting like a bunch of kids," he said, calling the boycotts "outrageous, absolutely outrageous."

"Security is more important than how hot the helmet will be or how much it makes everybody look alike."

"It will affect some people and not others," added Jim Ochowicz, the Motorola general manager. "Some people aren't affected by the heat and others are just going to melt away with that on their heads."

"That" is a rigid plastic shell with a liner of expanded polystyrene—also known as styrofoam—that crushes on impact, absorbing shock that would otherwise pass to the skull. Anchored by a chinstrap, the helmet can be reinforced with a Kevlar or nylon ring, and is covered with a thin plastic shell or a stretchy fabric cap to keep the helmet from breaking apart on impact. Costing usually between $75 and $100, the helmets worn by professionals are relatively lightweight, about 225 grams (8 ounces).

"I strongly believe in their use," said Greg LeMond, who has endorsed the Giro helmet since 1986. "There's a lot of risk involved in cycling, it's a very dangerous sport. I would advise anybody riding or training at almost any level to wear a helmet at almost all times.

"I don't want people to think I'm wearing a helmet just because I get paid to wear one," he continued. "I decide when to wear it, not my sponsor, and I wear it because I believe in safety.

"I used a helmet 90 percent of the time last year but I think it should be left to the rider's intelligence. There are times when they're not desirable and that's on a six-hour mountain stage in the Tour de France in 100-plus-degree weather.

"Regardless of any studies, you do six hours in 100-degree weather and a helmet's a lot hotter. One way of keeping the heat down on your body is dousing cold water over your head. How are you going to douse your head if you're wearing a helmet?

"Then there's recognition. For the television and spectators in the mountains, it's nice to see the suffering and the expressions on the riders' faces. It's probably what attracts many people to the sport."

Some of his feelings were echoed by many others, including Paul Sherwen, a former British rider who was now an official of the Motorola team. "Spectators go to see their own personal favorites and when you get a bunch of guys looking as if they're out of 'Star Wars,' you can't recognize anybody," he said. "When you have 200 guys with helmets and sunglasses, you don't recognize anybody."

Verbruggen scoffed at this. "It's the sunglasses," he felt. "I think it's a scandal to allow riders to wear their sunglasses even on the victory podium, hiding their faces to please their sponsors. We're not talking safety here, but money."

What the Basques Knew

The Basques got it right. Spanish and French, they turned out in the tens of thousands at Val Louron, the 13th stage, in hopes of celebrating a great Tour de France victory by one of their own.

Miguel Indurain responded, as he often has before in the Pyrenees, so close to his home. With a magnificent ride over five mountain peaks under a searing sun, he easily took over the yellow jersey. "Winning this jersey is my childhood dream," he said on the victory podium. "I'm confident that I'm not going to lose it in the Alps."

There were many big losers. Luc Leblanc, the overall leader at the start, struggled in more than 12 minutes late and fell to eighth place. Greg LeMond, who had no help from his team until the last 20 of the 232 kilometers, suffered a collapse nearly as total as Leblanc's. Racing at the end on courage alone, the American finished more than seven minutes behind Indurain.

LeMond looked crushed. His team's best support climbers, Robert Millar and Atle Kvalsvoll, were both hurt a week earlier in crashes and offered no help in the mountains. Nothing went right for LeMond. Already struggling on the next-to-last ascent, he was knocked down by a Gatorade support car for Gianni Bugno, but jumped up quickly and continued.

With nine daily stages remaining, including two full of climbing in the Alps, it was too early to say that Indurain had won the Tour or that LeMond had no chance left for his third successive victory. Still he was now 5 minutes 8 seconds behind, in fifth place overall, and plainly a weary racer.

Indurain was quite the opposite. He completed the last climb, a steep 6-kilometer ramp, with almost the same fluid stroke on his pedals that he exhibited at the start of the day. That said much about his condition since the stage topped five peaks.

Indurain, who celebrated his 27th birthday earlier in the week, handled them all with ease. He had experience, strength and an excellent Banesto team on his side. For all that, he had always before ridden in the service of Pedro Delgado, a condition that changed the moment Indurain swept across the finish line. Coming in, he swung an uppercut punch into the air: That was in joy, he explained, and an answer to all those who had questioned Banesto's strategy in waiting so long into the Tour before making its big move.

What was the point in not waiting? Indurain asked. Where else to take command of the race but the Pyrenees?

Heeding etiquette for a man gaining the yellow jersey, Indurain allowed his companion for the last two climbs, Claudio Chiappucci, to win the stage. The Italian jumped from 13th place overall to fourth, 4:06 back. Bugno was next across, 1:29 behind, followed by Laurent Fignon, then Charly Mottet, Andy Hampsten, Eduardo Chozas, Eric Boyer and LeMond.

The organizers of the Tour de France should strike a special medal for suffering and endurance and award it to all nine of them.

From the moment that Indurain attacked and opened a 55-second lead on the descent from the Tourmalet, the nine knew they were in the battle that would probably decide the entire race.

The lead mounted from the 55 seconds to 2:15 at the pass over the Aspin. From then on, the two leaders maintained their rhythm and only Bugno was able to reduce the margin at the end. LeMond faltered several times and was towed in by Boyer.

By the time LeMond finished, Indurain and his fans had long begun celebrating.

The Time of the Climbers

On the horizon, through a haze of heat, loomed the Pyrenees and their foothills. Now was the time of the climbers and, from experience, they all knew what confronted them. The mountains mean suffering.

Listen to a description by Ron Kiefel, a fine road captain for the Motorola team but a second-rank climber. "Your body hurts, your lungs hurt, you're breathing as hard as you can, you don't feel you can squeeze any more power out of your legs and you're just trying to settle down and get in a good rhythm," he says.

"If you go too easy, you can get dropped and finish outside the time limit." In that case, the rider is eliminated from the Tour.

And what if he goes too fast, trying to stay with such a strong climber as Pedro Delgado? "If I tried to climb with Delgado, I would blow up," Kiefel said. "I wouldn't make it to the finish line."

The suffering is only a little different for an accomplished climber, say Andy Hampsten of the Motorola team.

"My body is going so hard, my heart beating fast, breathing hard, my legs hurting," he said. "The trick is just accepting it and relaxing. I can accept the fact that my body is working way harder than it should."

Tour riders' bodies have worked harder since 1905, two years after the race began, when the first major climb, the Ballon d'Alsace, and two passes in the Alps were added to the itinerary. In 1910, came the Pyrenees.

Even a minor stage in the mountains is demanding. Take, for example, the stage from Pau to Jaca. The riders tackled passes over the Soudet Mountain, the Ichère and the Somport as they moved through the Pyrenees. The Soudet stands 1,540 meters high, the Ichère 680 meters and the Somport 1,640 meters. At its peak, any one of these climbs dwarfs the Empire State Building, which rises a mere 332 meters without its antenna and 381 with it.

Height is not the worst of it. The 23-kilometer (14-mile) climb up the Soudet included 6.4 kilometers with a grade of nearly 9 percent and 2.8 kilometers with a grade of 10 percent. The entire Samport climb of 18.7 kilometers had a grade of 5.6 percent.

Another way of measuring these mountains is by the scale used in bicycle races: from fourth category, the easiest climb, up to first category and then beyond—*hors catégorie*, beyond category in a combination of height, steepness, length of climb and, least, distance from the finish.

Thus the Soudet and Somport were both first category and the Ichère was second category.

Although the Alps and Pyrenees offer equally spectacular vistas and are both composed of calcium, a sedimentary rock, granite, an igneous rock, and gneiss, a metamorphic rock, the resemblance between them goes no further for bicycle racers. They judge by roads, not scenic beauty.

"The Pyrenees are a lot harsher," Kiefel feels. "They step up really quickly with very steep sections and then they flatten out. The roads are rougher.

"So it's a varied tempo when you climb. I like a steady tempo and that's what the Alps offer. They keep going up and keep going up. The percentages don't change very much, whereas in the Pyrenees you go from 3 to 4 percent and then you hit a 10-to-12 percent hill for a kilometer or two and then it flattens out. That really kills me."

Far more dangerous is the descent from a peak, which is usually as long and steep as the ascent but four times faster.

"I've never broken 100 kilometers an hour but I'm usually way into the 90s," Hampsten said. "Usually in the Tour we don't get going quite that fast because it's switchbacks and a lot of turns. It's faster in the Alps than in the Pyrenees because of the roads."

Descents are often made on roads that have no guard rails and that may be slick with water from glaciers melting atop the mountains. Or the roads may be slippery with loose gravel or soft with tar melted by the sun. Or any combination of these.

Nevertheless, Hampsten continued, his emotions are triggered less by the state of the descent than by his place in the long, strung-out pack.

"Sometimes I'm getting dropped and I'm completely terrified. And other times, when everything is going well, I flow down the mountain. Either I'm doing well, going on instinct, and I don't have any fear on the descent, or I'll be scared out of my mind every corner and nothing's working."

Kiefel, a lesser climber, cannot afford to be terrified on the descent. "We try to make up time on the descent," he said, speaking for himself and his peers, who try to stay together and pace each other in the leader's dust. On climbs, the riders call such a group 'a bus.'

Teammates are helpful in a bus. "You tell your teammate, 'Hey, I'm having a rough time, can you set the tempo for me and I'll follow you,'" Kiefel said.

For stronger riders, a teammate accompanying them on a climb is less useful than on the flat, where a leader can draft behind him and save up to 25 percent of the energy he would use if he were alone. Even if the draft is slight, every little bit helps. "If we're going 20 kilometers an hour uphill, the draft's not a big advantage," Hampsten said, "but after a couple of weeks of racing it's enough that you sure want to be behind somebody."

Show of Force

Did somebody mention the Italian Renaissance? After Claudio Chiappucci's victory for Carrera at Val Louron, it was time for the Ariostea team to flex its muscles: Bruno Cenghialta won the 14th stage, Moreno Argentin won the 15th and Marco Lietti won the 16th.

And who was that American who finished second to Lietti by two seconds after a long breakaway from Alès to Gap? Dispelling rumors that he was so sick or exhausted that he might have to quit, Greg LeMond nearly recorded a stage victory the day before the Alps were attacked at Alpe d'Huez.

For a while it seemed possible to believe again in LeMond's chances, but only for a while. The next day Miguel Indurain demonstrated all his considerable climbing strength and proved that he would be a tough man to overcome.

In the first, and presumably easier, of two stages in the Alps, Indurain finished a close second to Gianni Bugno, who used a powerful sprint at the finish to win at Alpe d'Huez for the second successive year. Indurain was a bicycle length and one second behind him, with the surprising Luc Leblanc another second behind.

Bugno was thrilled with his victory but put it into perspective. "It's going to be difficult to make up any time on Indurain, who's in excellent shape and has a terrific team," he said.

That was proven on the long climb to the peak as Jean-François Bernard, Indurain's teammate, set an explosive pace most of the way, faded and then managed to recover and finish fourth. Once Bernard was gone, Indurain easily stayed with Bugno, who kept looking back over his left shoulder to see if he was gaining ground. He wasn't.

The big losers on the day were LeMond and Charly Mottet, who ranked second before the stage. They both finished 1:58 behind Bugno. Somewhat lesser losers included Chiappucci, who finished 43 seconds behind, and Laurent Fignon, who finished 1:12 back.

When the computers had finished their work, they showed that Indurain led Bugno, in second place overall, by 3:09. Chiappucci was third, Mottet fourth and LeMond fifth, but 6:39 behind with time running out.

"I can't win this race," a saddened LeMond admitted afterward. "It's over now."

"Indurain's too strong," LeMond continued. He blamed his own problems on "a deep sense of fatigue" in his legs, discounting a viral infection from which, he said, he had suffered for three days. "Two days ago, if there would have been a mountain stage, I would have been out of the race," he said. After the infection was treated with antibiotics, "It's over now."

LeMond said he had scaled back his hopes for victory. "I hope to do a good time trial and maybe go top three" when the race finished. "It's one race, one time," he continued. Nevertheless, "It's hard to adjust to it," he said. "I'm not happy where I am but what can I do? I've been at such a point of fatigue since the Pyrenees it's impossible to come back, to be 100 percent now."

He doubted that he could somehow recover his best condition. "If there's a miracle, I might turn around overnight to become Superman," he said. "But there are no miracles in cycling," added the man who made up a 50-second deficit on the last day of the 1989 Tour to win by eight seconds.

CHAPTER 4

Black Clouds Ahead

One of the most perilous and exacting stages in the recent history of the Tour de France began in the tranquil village of Flumet, when those riders who happened to glance left could see black clouds building up over the distant Alps. A few moments later, the road curved sharply and the race headed directly toward the storm.

As the road mounted in the first major climb of the 18th stage, the air turned cold, a strong wind began to move the copses of ash trees on the mountainside and a sprinkle of rain began to fall. The nightmare had started.

More than four and a half hours later, Thierry Claveyrolat, the Eagle of Vizille, slogged in first across the finish line in Morzine. "I gave it everything I had," he said. Despite the horrendous weather, Claveyrolat was just one of many riders who finished half an hour ahead of the fastest clocking predicted by Tour organizers.

The reason was that time was running out for anybody hoping to take the yellow jersey from Miguel Indurain and this stage was one of the few remaining opportunities. But Indurain was not riding like a man who intended to be beaten. He finished 30 seconds behind Claveyrolat in the company of most other leaders except Greg LeMond, who lost nearly four minutes on the first major climb and struggled into the finish almost eight minutes late.

There were three major climbs: the Aravis Pass and the Colombière, both rated first category, and the Joux Plaine, rated beyond category. All, along with three hills on the itinerary, would have been difficult enough in hot weather; in a cold rain and fog, the climbs grew tortured and the speedy descents became a test of nerve, skill and equipment.

A seminar in descending was offered en route by Graham Jones, an Englishman who last rode the Tour in 1987 and now drove a car full of reporters.

"A light rain is worse for the riders than a heavy rain," Jones explained, "because a heavy rain at least washes all the motor oil off the road. A light rain leaves the road greasy. And a greasy road is not something you want to come down at top speed."

Nevertheless, any rider hoping to make up time on Indurain would have to take that chance.

"There should be big time gaps between groups or riders," Jones correctly predicted. The reason was that those riders who stormed down the descent would gain significant time on those who slowed to brake at each turn.

"You brake and the gap opens," Jones said. "Then you've got to work hard to catch up, and then there's another corner and another time to brake."

The rain was hardest atop the Colombière, where the riders grasped eagerly for light raincoats and for newspapers to stuff inside their jerseys as protection against the wind and cold on the way down. Like specters, the riders appeared out of the fog at the peaks and like specters they rode back into it. Only when Claveyrolat splashed across the finish line in the valley did the 161 riders who were left start to become mortal again.

The Picture of Victory

Sports psychologists call it "imaging:" a star athlete so vividly foresees himself throwing a touchdown pass or hitting a home run that he reacts with grace and confidence when he drops back to pass or steps into the batter's box.

Gert-Jan Theunisse knows about imaging.

For a year, he saw himself winning one of the two major alpine climbs in the 78th Tour de France. As he counted the days during a suspension from the sport for a year because of positive drug testing, Theunisse imaged himself first across the finish line at either Alpe d'Huez or Morzine. He had done it before, after all. In 1989 he was first up the climb to Alpe d'Huez, cementing his hold on the white jersey with red polka dots that goes to the king of the mountains.

Although a faraway look came across his face when he was asked about his vision, the Dutchman refused to say what he hoped to do in the Alps. "It means the same as every year," he insisted in a chat a few days before the mountains. Even Theunisse had to laugh at that. "I'll do my best," he promised, "and then we'll see."

His best was no better than good. At Alpe d'Huez he was 13th, one minute 58 seconds too slow. At Morzine he was fifth, 30 seconds too slow.

Theunisse, who ranked 13th overall, readjusted his goals once the Alps were past and said he now hoped to move up into the top 10. "That would be pretty good after a year away," he thought. "Besides, I was sick in the Pyrenees and you can't climb unless you're at your best. I had some bad orange juice in Spain and couldn't eat right afterward."

At his most lucid, Theunisse is a hard man to read. He can be playful but is most often brooding, with a wild glint in his eye. He would be a classic loner except for his devotion to Steven Rooks, another Dutchman and his former teammate and roommate with PDM and Panasonic.

"The Siamese twins," they were usually called. Even in 1991, when Theunisse rode for TVM and Rooks for Buckler, they and their wives remained close. "If I win in the Alps," Theunisse said before the race reached them, "I want Rooks to be right behind me. One, two, together." They last finished one, two at Alpe d'Huez in 1988, with Rooks first and Theunisse as happy as he was a year later when he won himself.

During the year that he was banned from the sport he spent a sum he estimated at $200,000 to clear his name. Doctors were consulted and tests run. He continued his daily training on the road, still taking along flasks that he filled with his urine for more tests.

His suspension lasted until June 12, 1991, when he won the first race he entered, the Tour of Luxembourg. A few weeks later he won another minor race, the Tour of the Mining Valleys in Spain.

While Theunisse was on the sidelines, Rooks was one of the very few riders who stood by him. He even traveled to the Canary Islands in the spring to help his friend up and down the hills there, paring his already lean body to 64 kilograms (140 pounds) with a remarkable body fat level of 4 percent, about half a racer's usual level.

Most of the rest of his year under suspension, Theunisse trained by himself.

Alpe d'Huez was his favorite training site. Theunisse climbed the 14 kilometers and 21 hairpin bends to the summit there 80 times.

Was he imaging himself at the front of a long line of riders strung down the mountainside? In his head, did he hear the hundreds of thousands of fans lining the road chant his name?

Theunisse dismissed the concept of imaging. He does not like to answer questions and, as he once said in a different context when he was happy, he never tells anybody his dreams.

Almost Over

With Miguel Indurain unbeatable, the Tour was heading toward its end and suddenly two Soviet riders—Dmitri Konichev of TVM and Slava Ekimov of Panasonic—snatched stage victories. The race had reached flat country again and the worst was over.

Then, with an admirable sense of symmetry, Miguel Indurain completed his domination of the Tour by easily winning a long individual time trial through the Burgundy countryside. Indurain, who increased his overall lead to 3 minutes 36 seconds before the ceremonial final stage into Paris, also won the first of two races against the clock.

"He's the strongest man in the race, that's for sure," Greg LeMond said later in tribute. "He deserves his victory."

Second in the time trial was Gianni Bugno, 27 seconds behind, and third was LeMond, 48 seconds behind.

At a news conference afterward, LeMond started by saying with a grin, "Finished, it's over—vacation. It's been a very difficult Tour de France for me, the most difficult I've had." He ranked seventh overall after the time trial, having passed Andy Hampsten, who dropped to eighth.

"I've learned that when you push yourself and win, it's much easier than when you push yourself and lose."

Then Indurain appeared and sat down next to LeMond. *"L'homme fort,"* the strong man, the American said. LeMond clapped the Spaniard, who does not understand French, on the shoulder and repeated the compliment in English, which Indurain does not understand either.

However, when LeMond pronounced him "the strongest man in the race," the beaming Indurain needed no translation.

The Final Yellow Jersey

Nearly a month before, Miguel Indurain had made a proud prediction to a mechanic with his Banesto team. "I'll win this Tour de France," Indurain said. "If I can't beat Greg LeMond this year, I'll quit racing forever."

The Spaniard fulfilled the vow, riding into Paris as the overwhelming winner. He took part in a final attack and then stayed clear of a crash in the sprint finish as the 158 remaining riders completed the 3,915-kilometer race.

Indurain recorded a total elapsed time of 101 hours one minute 20 seconds or 3 minutes 36 seconds less than Gianni Bugno in second place and 5:56 less than Claudio Chiappucci, who was third while winning the polka dot jersey of the best climber.

Charly Mottet, a Frenchman, was fourth and Luc Leblanc, another Frenchman, was fifth as the race reached its finale before hundreds of thousands of spectators in Paris. The last stage, 178 kilometers of rolling countryside and eight circuits of the Champs-Élysées, was won by Dmitri Konichev of TVM.

One rider who did not make it to the line was Djamolidine Abdoujaparov, the Uzbek who rode for Carrera and who had established himself as the fastest sprinter in the Tour while winning two stages and the green jersey of the points champion. Bearing down at the front of the sprint with perhaps 50 meters to go, Abdoujaparov hit a crowd barrier, crashed and somersaulted onto the road. Bruised and bloody, he was not seriously hurt although he was hospitalized.

For what is traditionally a ceremonial ride with many ritually unsuccessful attempts to break away on the Champs-Élysées, this was a thrilling finish except for the crash. Greg LeMond started the action by bolting off alone in the suburbs and his flight lasted until the third of the eight laps on the Champs-Élysées. Thereafter dozens of riders, in groups or alone, took their chances, fleeing like small boats from the tidal wave of the pack coursing behind them.

By the time the riders hung the final left at the Louvre and headed for the finish they were all together for the sprint, the crash, Konichev's second stage victory and Indurain's triumph.

His joy was evident even if he did not always articulate it. "Sometimes I suffer for him," says the Banesto team's manager, Francis Lafargue. "He has very strong feelings to express but he holds them in."

The victory was the fourth for Spain in the history of the race and first since Pedro Delgado won in 1988. The other Spanish winners were Luis Ocana in 1973 and Federico Bahamontes, the Eagle of Tolédo, in 1959.

October Again

And then it was again October, again time to unveil the Tour de France. The presentation began with a shock: Disregarding eight decades of tradition, the 1992 Tour de France would bypass the Pyrenees.

"We all know what the Tour owes to the Pyrenees," said Jean-Marie Leblanc, the Tour's racing director. "We love the Pyrenees and if we're not going there, it's not because we don't want to, it's because we can't."

The problem, he said, was the starting point, San Sebastián, Spain. The Basque city is close to the Pyrenees and the organizers decided that an immediate attack on the mountains was undesirable.

"If we'd gone there right from the start, we would have ruined interest in the race very early," Leblanc said, implying that many riders would lose so much time climbing the Pyrenees that they would have no further chance of winning the Tour.

As he presented the rest of the itinerary, Leblanc showed why the Tour would have no time for the Pyrenees: In covering 3,983 kilometers (2,490 miles) the Tour would spend time in each of seven European countries. That more than doubled the number any previous Tour had passed through.

The order, starting July 4 in San Sebastián, would be Spain, France, Belgium, the Netherlands, Germany, Luxembourg, France again and then Italy before the Tour returned definitively to France on July 19. The finish was scheduled for July 26 in Paris.

Leblanc explained that the international route had been chosen because 1992 was the year that the European Community planned to open its frontiers to the free circulation of goods, services and people.

"We could close our eyes to what is happening around us and stay with tradition or we could accept new ideas and innovations," he said. "All of us wanted the latter. We wanted to export the Tour to our closest neighbors and bring it right to the fans who now see us only on television."

So stages would finish in San Sebastián on July 4 and 5; in Brussels on July 10; in Valkenburg, the Netherlands, on July 11; in Koblenz, Germany, on July 12; in Luxembourg on July 13 and in Sestriere, Italy, on July 18.

Despite the loss of the Pyrenees, Leblanc insisted, mountains would not be neglected. The stage to Sestriere would be the first of two major days in the Alps, passing over five peaks including the 2,770-meter-high Iseran and the 2,083-meter-high Mont Cenis. On the next day, July 19, the Tour would again transit five mountains, including the 2,646-meter Galibier, the 1,670-meter Télégraphe and the 2,068-meter Croix de Fer, on the way to Alpe d'Huez.

Of those 10 climbs, Leblanc emphasized, five would be higher than 2,000 meters, or bigger than any climb in the 1991 race. Less strenuous climbing was scheduled July 15 in the Vosges mountains of eastern France and July 21 in the Massif Central.

On its clockwise way to the traditional finish on the Champs-Élysées, the Tour would pass within a few days' bicycle ride of the Pyrenees, but Leblanc said that no way could be found to go there within the three-week time limit. The closest the 198 riders from 22 teams would come was the ascension of the minor Marie Blanque pass on the road from San Sebastián to Pau on July 6.

"But we're not crazy," Leblanc added. "We'll be back in the Pyrenees next year."

Reaction was mixed when Leblanc finished his presentation.

"I can't say I like it," said Roger Legeay, the coach of the Z team based in France and a former Tour rider himself. "The Tour de France ought to be a little more about France, I think, and the Pyrenees are what the race is made of." He was echoed by Stephen Roche. "The Tour without the

Pyrenees is like Paris-Roubaix without the cobblestones," the Irishman said.

Others were less critical. "If you think the Pyrenees have been left out, you haven't had to climb the Marie Blanque," said Bernard Hinault, who had to climb it many times on his way to five victories in the Tour.

As for the race itself, Legeay thought it would suit his team leader, Greg LeMond. "It looks tougher than the last one," Legeay judged, "and Greg likes it tough."

Roche and Miguel Indurain agreed that the next edition looked difficult.

"More mountains," said Roche. "More and bigger mountains."

Long time trials, said Indurain. In addition to the short prologue, 8 kilometers, on July 4, there would be a team time trial over 63 kilometers on July 8 and two individual time trials—over 65 kilometers on July 13 and over 64 kilometers on July 24. In a switch, the team time trial was moved to a day of its own, before a long plane flight to the next stage, rather than being scheduled as a half stage the day after the prologue.

The multinationalization of the race meant that in addition to the Pyrenees, the bicycle-mad region of Brittany would be skipped. Press reaction there was predictably anguished: "The Tour is no longer the Tour de France," cried the *Courrier de l'Ouest*. "Now it's no more than a trademark, something exportable wherever it can be sold. The local train that used to visit every corner of France has become a cold and distant Trans-European Express."

CHAPTER 5

Another Tour

A Man of Modest Goals

Gino De Backer had modest goals as a bicycle racer, perhaps because, at age 29 and in his fourth year as a professional, he had just one victory to his credit. That occurred in 1990 in a kermesse, or one of the many minor races held in and around villages in the Low Countries. The place was Desselgem, Belgium, not far from his home in Destelbergen.

Before that, De Backer's main achievement was a fifth place in the 1988 Paris–Tours race, a World Cup classic. His dark face breaks into a sunny smile when he remembers the sprint finish in Paris–Tours and the cheers of tens of thousands of spectators lining the straightaway to the finish line.

By now the Belgian had learned that most professional riders are measured by more than the cheers of the crowd. If they ride, as De Backer did, for the B squad of a second-echelon team like Tonton Tapis in a race as distant from home base in Belgium as the 1991 Tour Du Pont, honors are what count.

But De Backer had no hope, absolutely none, of winning the Tour Du Pont and carrying off the $50,000 that went to the victor. Nor could he realistically dream of winning a daily stage ($800) or the championships for sprinters ($1,000), climbers ($2,000) or even best young riders ($1,000).

At mile 49 of the stage from Richmond to Wintergreen, Virginia, De Backer saw his chance at an attainable goal, however modest.

"I hoped to win the jersey of the most aggressive rider," he explained hours later. So De Backer attacked. Of the 102 other riders, all remained indifferent except for Dave Spears of Team Canada, an amateur. Not bothering to chase, the pack watched placidly as Spears sprinted after and joined De Backer. Helped by a crash that blocked the pack briefly, the two quickly disappeared on the rolling and twisty road.

Twenty miles later, their lead was up to 7 minutes 30 seconds, its peak. The pack had passed through a feed zone by then and been slowed by the usual confusion as riders snatched their lunches on the fly and transferred sandwiches, pastries and fruits from small sacks to the pockets of their jerseys.

That accomplished, a desultory chase began. Neither De Backer nor Spears was dangerous—the Belgian ranked 59th, the Canadian 70th at the start of the day—but various teams' tactics dictated that the road ahead be clear by the final climb to the resort of Wintergreen.

The focus should have been on De Backer but, for his hour of glory, he chose an empty stage. The backroads from Richmond were bordered by nothing but untended and overgrown fields, many of them unfenced. Houses were rare and spectators even rarer. At the few crossroads, state policemen were posted to hold back traffic that had not arrived. Only at a bonus sprint in the town of Scottsville did a small crowd gather, and there Spears was first across the line.

"Nobody," De Backer remembered later. Nobody to witness his feat.

He and Spears relayed each other through eerily empty Virginia, passing stands of loblolly pine, ash and maple. Sidewinds stirred tulip trees and fields of blackeyed Susans: Still life with bicycle racers.

And their lead was coming down.

By mile 78, it was 3 minutes 40 seconds and, despite their steady pace, by mile 80, it was 3:15. By mile 88, when the two began climbing a long hill, the lead was barely 2 minutes. Spears was stroking easily on the climb while De Backer began to struggle. He was soon left behind.

"I felt good," De Backer recalled. "The other guy, he didn't want to wait. He wanted to go alone, he said goodbye.

"An amateur," De Backer said contemptuously.

He was quickly swallowed up by the pack, which continued after Spears.

A few minutes after De Backer was caught, Spears reached the the town of Faber, an outpost of civilization. Alone he raced past a post office, the Mount Shiloh Baptist Church, the Faber Volunteer Fire Company, a line of train tracks leading to some big city somewhere.

People were out and cheering.

As he turned onto Highway 29 South, traffic was backed up for a few hundred yards and drivers had left their cars to watch. Applause and shouts of encouragement greeted the Canadian as he passed the Meander Inn and the Stoney Creek Golf Course.

And then, of course, it was Spears's turn to be caught. At the finish, he was 10:39 behind the winner. De Backer labored in 17:31 behind at the mountain top.

"My legs were good on the climb," De Backer said, "but my coach said to me, 'Easy, easy, there's another race tomorrow.' I've got a chance there if I make it over the hills, then maybe on the flat or in the sprint."

He was pleased with himself and his performance, but curious.

Had he won the prize as most aggressive rider? he wondered. "I think not," he said, since he had not been notified.

It seemed kinder not to tell him that the honor had been voted instead to Spears.

Numero Uno

From his butcher's stall in the Calle de Erbieta municipal market in San Sebastián, Spain, Paco Echeverria was happy to talk *chuletas, bistecas* and even *hamburguesas*, but what he seemed happiest to talk were *bicicletas*.

As in *ciclismo*, as in the 1992 Tour de France. It was to begin in San Sebastián in a few days and Paco Echeverria was prepared to recommend a few choice cuts among the riders.

"Indurain," he said, *"Muy bueno."* Several large posters of Miguel Indurain adorned the walls behind the butcher's counter.

Echeverria jerked a bandaged thumb toward some of the other posters. "Bugno," he said, "LeMond, Breukink *muy peligroso."*

That was prime rib; Gianni Bugno, Greg LeMond and Erik Breukink figured to be very dangerous indeed to Indurain's hopes in the three-week Tour.

The butcher shook his head in decision. "Indurain," he said, *"Numero uno."*

Even a lactoid vegetarian would find it hard to argue with this verdict. At that moment, Indurain ranked first among the world's professional bicycle racers and had just recorded two impressive victories. First, in mid-June, he became the first Spaniard to win the Giro d'Italia and then, a week before the start of the Tour, he overtook a three-man breakaway and won the sprint to become Spanish national champion. (For commercial and political reasons, including reluctance to inflame Basque passions, Indurain did not wear the Spanish national champion's jersey in the Tour. He sported instead a small Spanish insignia on his Banesto team jersey.)

The victory in the Spanish championships was bad news for his rivals in the Tour, who had hoped that Indurain lost it in the Giro. "It" was the untiring power that makes him a top climber and the master of the long time trial.

This 79th Tour seemed to be designed for him. It included two days of major climbs in the Alps and two long time trials on either side of those mountains. But the soft-spoken— sometime so soft that he seems to be nearly inarticulate— Indurain was not claiming victory beforehand. He was, in fact, trying to sound cautionary.

"The fact that I'll start with No. 1 on my back and wearing the yellow jersey in my own country will mean a lot," he said in an interview with local organizers. "That was one of my first thoughts last year in Paris: That I would be in yellow in San Sebastián. But they'll also add to the pressure on me. It's going to be very difficult."

That was consistent with the wariness he had displayed since his Giro victory.

"In the Tour, experience has taught me that you never do anything the way you do it in another race," he told the French daily *l'Équipe* after his victory in Italy.

Asked if he could bring off the Giro-Tour double, he replied enigmatically, "It could be just as easy, if I ride the way I did in the Giro, as it could be difficult."

The double victory in the same year would put him in elite company. Only Fausto Coppi in 1952, Jacques Anquetil in 1964, Eddy Merckx in 1970, '72 and '74, Bernard Hinault in 1982 and '85, and Stephen Roche in 1987 had managed it.

"I'm in form," Indurain continued, "I've worked hard, I won the time trials in the Giro, I climbed well, but I'm no Superman. I don't feel stronger than LeMond or Bugno. The Tour is so difficult.

"But the Giro victory gives me a lot of confidence, especially when you can finish feeling good, not tired."

Even before the Giro finished, Indurain displayed that confidence. A reporter for *l'Équipe* noted that each time a rival attacked in Italy, the Spaniard overtook him and stared him down. Was that arrogance? Indurain was asked. "No," he replied, "it was a matter of principle. I was wearing the pink jersey and I wanted to show them that I was the boss. I never bluffed."

His Giro victory was overwhelming, including victory in the last day's time trial by 2 minutes 46 seconds. The final general classification showed Claudio Chiappucci of Carrera in second place by 5:12, with Franco Chioccioli of GB-MG Boys third, 7:16 behind, Marco Giovannetti of Gatorade fourth, 8:01 behind, and Andy Hampsten of Motorola fifth, 9:16 behind.

Such havoc left the oldtimers cheering. "I've never seen a Spaniard like him," said Felice Gimondi, the last Italian to win the Tour, nearly three decades ago. Other Spaniards, he explained, rode on instinct. "Indurain, on the other hand, calculates everything he's going to do. He has an exceptional sense of the race."

Merckx agreed. "He's the strongest and the smartest," he said of Indurain. "He's my favorite for the Tour."

Off to a Bad Start

Greg LeMond insisted that he did not believe in omens and that was just as well for him as the Tour de France began.

For one omen, LeMond finished 15th in the prologue. For another omen, the prologue was won by Miguel Indurain. A final omen could serve as a training tip from the top: The best way to arrive at the Tour de France is not in a state of near-collapse.

"I'm nervous, I'm stressed out, I'm exhausted before I even start the Tour," LeMond complained the day before the prologue. He was also a little overweight, might have had a cold and felt dehydrated.

LeMond had just spent a harrowing two days in traveling from his home in Belgium to the Spanish northeast. Blockaded frontiers, plane strikes, television appearances, training rides, cars that ran out of gas, among other plagues, stretched his journey out from what should have been 10 hours.

"Basically I spent 36 hours traveling to get here," LeMond noted in his hotel in San Sebastián. "I'll be OK in the prologue," he predicted, more or less accurately since he finished ahead of 183 other riders. "I'm sure I'll be OK. Everybody tries to win the prologue. You go all out, you can't hold back."

He tried to be as good as his word in the 8 kilometer (5-mile) prologue as, holding nothing back, he rode strongly enough into blustery winds to gain his 15th place.

Indurain held less than nothing back. In front of hundreds of thousands of his fans, he finished in 9 minutes 22 seconds and 43 hundredths of a second. His time was two seconds better than that of Alex Zuelle, a Swiss who rides for the ONCE team, who was second. LeMond clocked 9:36.91.

Indurain's victory on a course that snaked through San Sebastián set off loud and friendly celebrations from the half-moon bay of La Concha, just off the start, to the tidal Urumea River alongside the finish.

And so began the 79th Tour de France, which started in 1903 and has been stopped only by both world wars. In recent years, however, the race has sometimes been disrupted, as was happening again. Early on the morning of the prologue, Basque terrorists firebombed press cars in an outlying town. The attack followed an incident of arson and an attempted firebombing directed at the Tour in San Sebastián. When the race crossed into France in two days, protesting truck drivers were expected to try to disrupt the Tour to get some publicity for their cause.

LeMond had already run up against the truckers, whose northern battle corps sealed the border from Belgium on his trip to Spain.

But, as he said when asked if his traveling problems had been a bad omen, "No way. Actually when things go bad for me, they get better soon afterward.

"I really feel OK, I was just exaggerating," he insisted. "It was frustrating to have to go through all that before the most important race there is."

For LeMond, after his seventh place in 1991, there were many challenges ahead. He knew it and thought he knew how to deal with them. His mood seemed quietly confident and he reported that his condition was fine. Other people on his Z team, which is based in France, confirmed that he was ready and able to seek his fourth Tour victory.

That went against the consensus that Indurain was unbeatable, LeMond noted.

"Most people consider me an outsider with little chance of winning," he said. "A contender," he added scornfully. "It's a little ridiculous to me but puts a lot of pressure on the other riders and gives me a little more freedom.

"I'm going to race like everybody's saying—a contender. That means I'm not going to have my team chase down breakaways. Indurain is going to have to take control of this race if he wants to win it for a second time.

"He might be too strong to do anything about, who knows? But he might not be. He's beatable, anybody's beatable, given the right moment."

Among the ranks of the beatable was LeMond himself. "Last year taught me that I can lose the Tour," he admitted. "Last year I had a two-and-a-half minute lead and I wanted to make sure nobody got that back before the mountains," he explained. "That wasted a lot of energy.

"And so I have to race, not a little smarter—I think I've always raced the Tour de France very smart—but more conservatively."

He weighed 70 kilograms (154 pounds) and hoped to lose one or two of them in the early stages of the Tour.

"That extra weight is the only thing that kept me back from winning the Dauphiné Libéré and the Tour of Switzerland," he said, referring to his two most recent stage races. He was 11th in the Dauphiné and fourth in the Tour of Switzerland.

"One or two kilos, you know how much difference they make on a hill?" he asked, using the racers' self-reassuring word for a mountain.

Still, he said, "My condition is very high. Last year, in the Tour of Switzerland, I was lighter and not climbing nearly as well as this year. I suffer a little on the hills but I think everybody does.

"Last year, after the Tour de France, I felt fatigued. This year, after every stage race, I felt better, which is like my normal self. I just need to improve a little bit. I'll find that improvement between now and the Alps, I'm certain."

LeMond was looking weary and still had a training ride ahead before he could rest.

It was time for him to go, but he sat and thought once more about the Tour de France.

"A contender," he finally snorted.

Going for the Gold Ring

Chasing his big dream, Eddie B. is in France today. He was in Switzerland yesterday, in Italy the day before and he will head for Germany tomorrow. "Everybody is dreaming about something, I'm dreaming too," he explains. "I'm dreaming big dream."

Vast dream, really. Eddie Borysewicz, who is universally known as Eddie B. because Americans could not pronounce his name when he arrived 15 years ago from his native Poland, built the U.S. amateur cycling program that won handfuls of medals at the 1984 Olympic Games in Los Angeles. "When I started, was nothing," he remembers. "No office, nothing. I was the first guy, who don't speak English. I have only a telephone and have even to buy a desk. That was '78, OK? We make big steps. I have so many riders who win the Olympics, world championship medals."

Now, at age 53 in 1992, after his highly successful career teaching amateurs, Eddie B. was in his first year as a professional directeur sportif, dreaming of competing soon in the Tour de France.

"So far, so good, extremely good, even more than I expected," he says of his Subaru-Montgomery Securities team. "Nice bunch of guys, enthusiastic. These guys not complain. Our results are good and everybody is surprised how well we go. That does not mean we have no problems— we have a lot of problems." (One of them is that just when his English grew rapid and picturesque in its shortcuts, everybody else began speaking Spanish or Italian or French, which he has not used in 15 years.)

Undaunted, Eddie B. dreams his dream: He will build the best team in the sport, and he will do it soon. "We're going to be the top team in the world," he says flatly. Top team? "Top team. We need for this a couple of years and we need luck."

Also money, victories, more staff, more experience, more than his current dozen road riders, more time in the day—the list of 'mores' is a long one, headed by more money. In a sport dominated by teams that spend at least $5 million a year, Eddie B. had a budget of $1.4 million.

"It sounds like a lot of money if you don't know much about professional cycling," says one of his riders, Rob Holden. "If you do understand the sport, you know what a small budget it is."

Holden was speaking at the team's hotel in Nantes, France, where, like his coach, he arrived after driving two days with two teammates from a race in Italy. Although they stayed in a sponsor's hotels along the way, the riders looked tired. "Drive, that's us, that's what we can do," Eddie B. said. "That's not Buckler, OK, that's not Panasonic," referring to two Dutch teams with the money for plane fares to races and luxurious private buses.

Star riders for those teams were in Italy that weekend, racing the Milan–San Remo classic, which began in 1907. The smaller fry were in western France, preparing to ride Cholet–Pays de Loire, which began in 1978 and which bills itself as the first French classic of the season, defining a classic not as a venerable and prestigious race but merely as a one-day event. People more disinterested than the race's promoters would rank Cholet–Pays de Loire as a semi-classic.

Whatever its standing, Cholet–Pays de Loire offered—in reduced amounts—just what the hallowed Milan–San Remo did: money, publicity and points in the riders' computerized standings. For the many teams that did not have the money or points to enter Milan–San Remo, Cholet–Pays de Loire was an opportunity to race, to get a foot on a low rung of the ladder and begin ascending.

So such barely known professional teams as Collstrop, Assur Carpets and La William journeyed from Belgium. Cermia represented Spain, Pro Road Project Japan, Chazal and Eurotel France and Subaru-Montgomery the United States. "We're an American team based in America with American sponsors and some American riders," Eddie B. said. "Also some European riders. I think we well represent Subaru, Montgomery Securities and America, OK? To have another American team present in Europe and doing well, that will help American cycling grow."

Despite its American roots, his team planned to compete almost exclusively in Europe. A major reason is that the points a team needs for big races are more readily available in Europe than in the United States. They were known as FICP points from the initials in French of the International Federation of Professional Cycling.

"Without FICP points, nothing," Eddie B. points out. "We're collecting FICP points and we're learning." Already his team had won enough points in races in France and Italy to advance from 40th in the world to 27th. The top 20 teams automatically qualify for World Cup races and the top 16 for the Tour de France, Subaru's major goal.

But not for 1992. "This is a testing year: What can we do? What can the riders do? What kind of experience do we need?" Eddie B. asks.

"This is a learning experience for me. I'm learning about professional cycling. It's new for me. I can make several mistakes this year that I will eliminate next year.

"Next year is going to be our real season in Europe. We did not come from nowhere, we are not nobodies. We are already a very competitive team. Next year we'd like to be in the Tour de France and I believe we will be in the Tour de France.

"Only we need a little bit more money. We need a doubled budget. We're not looking for $5 million or $8 million like the big teams. For $3 million we can produce results like big teams. Because we're hard workers.

"I need more people, I need more money. The problem is money limits your life. I need another directeur sportif, I need four mechanics instead of one, four masseurs instead of one. Masseur doesn't speak English, which is a big problem since masseur is like mother after the race and needs to understand English-speaking riders."

Lacking money, Eddie B. turns to friends and contacts he has made in his many years in the sport. An official of the French Cycling Federation helped him hire Denis Roux, one of the team's more experienced riders but one left without a job when his Toshiba team folded in 1991. A doctor for the Italian Cycling Federation monitors Subaru riders' health. A friend in Dortmund, Germany, supplies offices, storage space and a phone number for race promoters to call. "Without help like this, we can't survive," Eddie B. says.

Immediately after the Cholet race, he adds, he plans to drive to his headquarters in Germany. Another problem. "I need to be in Dortmund and in Belgium at the same time to talk to agent and sign the contract for next races."

Races mean start money. For a small race, Cholet–Pays de Loire paid what it could. "Little money," Eddie B. says, "5,500 francs" or about $1,400. He even considered dropping out of the race because two of his better riders— Roux and Mike Carter, formerly of Motorola — were sidelined with knee tendinitis and the others were tired. The penalty for breach of contract, however, was 10,000 francs, which he decided was too steep.

Subaru Montgomery would race, but with limited goals. "Tomorrow please don't expect very good results from us," he cautioned. "Only riders who have a chance to be top 10 have to finish. Others can stop when they want. We're taking this race as a warm up."

Outside the hotel, in the chill evening, his team mechanic was struggling to fit a bicycle rack atop a car. Eddie B. noticed this and went to help, tugging the rack into place and trying to tighten its bolts. Not many directeurs sportifs have to bother with chores like that, he was told.

"I worked like this when I started in American cycling," he replied, hammering the rack with his right hand. "I made some history in amateur cycling and right now I try to do my best in professional cycling. My disadvantage is I don't know races. I am learning about these races. But that's nice. Next year I'm going to have different experience."

The next morning, Subaru-Montgomery showed up not only with limited goals but also with one of the smaller teams in the 18-team race: Only five of its riders mounted the podium in the windswept Place General de Gaulle in Cholet and signed in as several hundred spectators clapped intermittently.

"The American team, Subaru," intoned the race announcer, Daniel Mengeas, usually a warehouse of minutiae about riders. This time he was stumped. Eddie B. had entered Nate Reiss, who had ridden almost exclusively in the United States; Rob Holden and Chris Walker, who had ridden almost exclusively in England; Martin Aun, an Estonian who rode almost exclusively nowhere but was so eager that he competed for expenses only, and Janus Kuum, a Norwegian who was born in Estonia. Mengeas perked up when he spotted Kuum, who has raced for a handful of European teams and thus had a history that could be acclaimed.

First to report, Subaru-Montgomery set a bad precedent for the announcer. The major teams in the race—Lotto, Castorama, Z, RMO, PDM, Lotus, Buckler, Tulip, Helvetia and GB-MG Boys—all sent B squads packed with young, unknown riders, while reserving their stars for Milan–San Remo. The minor teams—Chazal, Eurotel, Cermia, Pro Road Project, La William, Collstrop and Assur Carpets— sent their A squads but these riders had few glories to be sung; if they had more, the riders would have been invited to join major teams. As one nonperson after another trooped on stage, Mengeas wilted.

Then, to the blare of horns as team cars tried to form a line, the riders mounted their bicycles and the race freewheeled out of town. The real starting point was 7 kilometers away, where a herd of black and white cows gazed forlornly at the 143 riders. They set off uneventfully and only the changing color of pastured cows—now brown and white, now mostly black, back to black and white— proved that time was passing.

Chatting with his mechanic, Alain Denegre, in the back seat and a guest in the front seat, Eddie B. worked to maintain his position in the long line of team cars. He had drawn No. 4 out of the hat and pronounced it lucky for obscure reasons. Its real advantage was that he was close enough behind the pack to see quickly if any of his riders needed help.

For that reason, different directeurs sportif, those with numbers in the teens, kept trying to jump the line. The biggest offender was the canny Cyrille Guimard of Castorama, whose number was so high that he violated the rules and failed to post it in his car's rear window. That way, perhaps, nobody would realize he was cutting in.

At kilometer 12, the radio linking team cars reports a crash ahead. Eddie B. quickly stops and Denegre leaps out, carrying two replacement wheels, but just as quickly returns and reports no Subarus involved. At kilometer 15, a rider jumps away from the pack and builds a lead of more than a minute. Eddie B. does not worry. "One rider not dangerous," he decrees. "Five serious, 10 dangerous but one, no problem. Too much headwind today." He admires the point of the breakaway, however. "Good publicity for team. When someone is not good, not going to finish, smart thing to do."

Kilometer 17: Reiss drifts to the rear of the pack and raises his right hand, asking for help. He wants to pass to the car three jackets that Subaru riders have taken off as they begin to work up a sweat.

91

"Nate, PDM and Lotto are talking," Eddie B. warns. "The cars pull alongside and they talk. Maybe friendly talk, 'How are you?' maybe making a deal. If they move to front, watch out. Tell the boys."

Reiss nods and the car drops back. "Warning never hurts," Eddie B. says. Guimard again tries to cut in front.

Kilometer 26: A Japanese rider for Pro Road Project has been dropped on the first climb and struggles to get back to the pack. "Position terrible," Eddie B. judges. "A tourist would look better. Only 26 km and already absolutely dead.

"Maybe sick," he adds charitably.

Kilometer 33: "There's my boy," Eddie B. shouts, gunning the motor, as a rider far ahead pulls over to the right side of the road with a flat. When he draws nearer, Eddie B. realizes that the rider is from Eurotel, which wears the same day-glo yellow hat as Subaru. The car drops back.

Kilometer 40: Walker asks for help and passes his jacket in. "Stay at front, my friend," he is told.

Kilometer 80: Holden calls for help. "I can't turn the pedals," he says. A 14-man breakaway has developed and left the other riders split into small groups, fighting strong crosswinds. "You can't go, drop out at feed zone," Eddie B. says. Then he races off to see if any Subaru riders are in the breakaway. He doubts it since the radio has not mentioned his riders' numbers but race radios are not always accurate. Besides, Subaru has drawn numbers in the 90s and the French for Walker's 97—four twentys, ten seven—is too complicated for Eddie B.'s rusty skills. Among the decipherable numbers are two riders from the Castorama team—11 through 20—directed by Guimard. His car has long deserted the line, as it is allowed to do if a team has riders in a breakaway.

Kilometer 98: Eddie B. pulls up to another large group of riders and counts two more Subarus. If there is only one group ahead, he has two men up among the leaders, fighting for prize money and points, which go to the first 10 riders. "We have to go!" Eddie B. announces, making his car jump the curb and speeding on the sidewalk to get past riders spread across the road as they battle the wind. Just before he hits a road sign, Eddie B. whips the car back onto the road, ahead of the riders. "Sometimes like that," he says, "but it's my boys."

Kilometer 128: Finally the team car reaches the next bunch of riders, including Reiss and Aun. "A bunch went and I tried to bridge over with two Castoramas and a Zed but the Castoramas wouldn't work," Reiss reports. "We could have made it if they worked."

"Better 2 in the top 14 than 4 in the top 40," Eddie B. says, meaning that if the Castorama riders had cooperated in trying to overtake the leaders, they might have towed along the whole chasing pack. "That's racing—miss the break, you miss it. Like life." He consoles Reiss. "It's over," he says. "You did good." The chasing group slows, knowing it cannot overhaul the leaders. By the time Laurent Des-biens of Collstrop reaches Cholet and easily wins the race, the chasers are far behind. Aun is the only finisher for Subaru, 25 minutes back.

Somewhere on the slow trip to town, his guest tells Eddie B. that it wasn't surprising Castorama led the attack and refused to chase: The sponsor, a chain of hardware stores, is especially popular in this part of France and Guimard comes from nearby Nantes.

Eddie B. thinks about this. "I didn't know," he says. "Too bad you didn't tell me before so I tell them to watch Castorama."

And he says, "That's education. I'll remember that next year."

The Heart of Basque Country

The Sanchez furniture store in the Plaza de Zaragoza in San Sebastián had a front window packed with bicycle jerseys, caps and posters, including a giant one of Miguel Indurain on the victory podium in Paris after he won the 1991 Tour de France.

The Kasvi barber shop on the Alameda del Boulevard had in its window one of the leader's yellow jerseys that Indurain wore on his way to Paris.

On the Calle de Reina Regente, a bakery had a huge photograph of the Basque rider Marino Lejaretta in a yellow jersey, which he wore briefly a few years back. Also in the window were two signs with the battle cry "Aupa" flanked by somersaulting exclamation points in the Spanish manner.

A delicatessen in the Avenida Felipe IV displayed the work of an artist in the neglected medium of cold cuts. He had mapped, in chorizo, the route of the 79th Tour de France.

In short, San Sebastián had taken *El Tour* to its bosom. That was not surprising, since the Basques of northeastern Spain love cycling and boasted a dozen riders in the Tour and 23 amateur bicycle clubs in the three Basque provinces. That love is the reason San Sebastián was willing to pay $1 million to be host to the Tour on its first visit there since a one-day stage in 1949.

The charming seaside city of 180,000 residents is part of the heart of the Basque country, perhaps the aorta. On Stage One, the Tour traveled 194.5 kilometers (121 miles) through the auricles and ventricles.

At the finish of the race into and past the cities and pueblos of Guipúzcoa Province, the winner was Dominique Arnould, a 25-year-old Frenchman with the Castorama team from France. Second, half a bicycle length behind, was Johan Museeuw of the Lotto team from Belgium and third was Max Sciandri, an Italian with the Motorola team from the United States.

In his excitement at having held off the pack after a breakaway, Arnould raised his right arm in victory less than 10 meters from the finish. He then glanced back, saw a horde of riders bearing down on him and resumed racing, not coasting. Museeuw was not quite able to catch the Frenchman.

Although all the favorites finished in the same time, the overall leader's yellow jersey changed hands. Miguel Indurain dropped to second place behind Alex Zuelle, who won a bonus intermediate sprint and gained six seconds that were deducted from his overall elapsed time. Zuelle had been second by two seconds to Indurain in the prologue.

That foreigners finished first, second and third in the first stage was fitting. San Sebastián is Blanche Dubois country: kindness to strangers is as native to the Basque as to the bedouin.

Yet many native hearts must have yearned for another victor. Marino Lejaretta, for example, the man in the yellow jersey in the bakery's photograph.

As he said, he was still dreaming of victory as recently as that spring. A victory before his fellow Basques in the province next to his own Vizcaya would have capped his last season as the undisputed strongman, the iron horse, of professional bicycle racing.

But in mid-April, not long before his 35th birthday, Lejaretta crashed heavily in a race outside nearby Bilboa. When he awoke in a hospital, he had broken ribs, a punctured lung and fractured vertebrae in his back. His career was over, except for two farewell races late in the fall.

Now a guest of honor of the Tour de France, his role was limited to cutting the ceremonial ribbon for Stage One. This was the first Tour de France Lejaretta had not ridden in since 1985. It was, in fact, one of the few of the three grand

Tours he had missed since then. For the last three years he had ridden in the Giro d'Italia, the Vuelta de Espana and the Tour de France—a total of about 7,000 miles from each mid-May through each July.

All told, he rode 11 Vueltas, 7 Giros and 8 Tours. He rode them well too, finishing fifth in the 1989 and 1990 Tours de France, fifth in the 1991 Giro and third in the Vuelta the same year. His big victory was the 1982 Vuelta.

The only other rider who had ridden in all three Tours for three consecutive years was Bernando Ruiz of Spain, who did it in 1955, '56 and '57. Nowadays, a rider who tackles two of the Tours in the same year is considered to be a workaholic.

Lejaretta did not ride mainly the Tours once he turned professional in 1979. He competed in nearly every race possible in the eight-month calendar and rode them well. Among his 56 victories were two Tours of Catalonia and three times the Grand Prix of San Sebastián.

Like Zuelle, the new wearer of the yellow jersey, Lejaretta rode for the team sponsored by ONCE, the Organizacion Nacional de Ciegos Espanoles, or national federation for the blind. Among other jobs, they staff lottery booths throughout Spain, selling tickets and making change by feeling the size and texture of peseta banknotes.

A huge ONCE poster at several strategic spots in Basque country showed a sightless man wearing a racing jersey and sitting alongside a bicycle. Above his head, the poster said, "The Other Marino." It was both mawkish and touching.

Traveling the stage in an organization car as an honored guest, not a racer, the original Marino surely understood that feeling.

Through an ancient arch, the Tour de France pack travels from the Pyrenees toward the Alps.

Facing page: Domestique at work: Andy Bishop fetching musettes for his Motorola team.

Above: At the start of the 1991 Tour, Greg LeMond is the center of attention.

Below: A splash of local color as the Tour passes through Brittany.

Facing page: Claudio Chiappucci, first at Val Louron—but with Miguel Indurain right behind him.

Above: Thierry Marie of Castorama riding to victory after his 234 km solo breakaway.

Below: Australian rider Phil Anderson wins the stage into Quimper.

Above: Sent packing. The PDM bus and a team car being loaded with riders' suitcases and bicycles after the team's withdrawal from the '91 Tour following a mysterious illness.

Below: The broom wagon, or voiture balai, brings up the rear in the Tour de France. By 1992, the broom was inside.

Above: Unable to stay with the leaders, Greg LeMond struggles in the Pyrenees.

Below: Laurent Fignon sets the pace through a storm on the climb to Morzine.

Above: At the conclusion of the 1991 Tour, Djamolidine Abdoylaparov, ahead in the sprint, hits a barrier and crashes while the pack rushes by him.

Below: Luis Ocaña, winner of the 1973 Tour, chats with Miguel Indurain.

Facing page: Miguel Indurain starts the 1992 Tour by winning the prologue in San Sebastian.

Above: Jean-François Bernard paces his teammate Indurain, center, and Gianni Bugno, left, up to the Alpe d'Huez.

Below: José-Miguel Echavarri, directeur sportif of the Banesto team and Indurain's mentor.

Above: Miguel Indurain in the yellow jersey.

Below: At the conclusion of the '91 tour, the Banesto team, riders and officials, take a victory lap on the Champs-Elysées.

Chased uphill? Cattle crossing amid the high pastures of the Alps.

Above: Miguel Indurain at the center of activity in the team time trial.

Below: An old trick: hitching a ride on a photographer's motorcycle.

Above: Italian fans encourage, not to say impede, Claudio Chiappucci in the Alps.

Below: At Sestriere, Chiappucci duplicates Fausto Coppi's victory decades earlier.

Above: In the first 1992 time trial, Indurain passes Laurent Fignon.

Below: Heading toward the finish in Paris, the tour passes through the château country of the Loire Valley.

Above: The strung-out pack heads up the Champs Elysées toward the Arc de Triomphe and the finish of the Tour.

Below: At the finish of the 1992 Tour, Indurain is congratulated by two admirers.

Into the Homeland

The Tour de France bid *adios* to Spain, land of fiesta and siesta, and returned to its homeland in a peculiar fashion for Stage Two. For the first time since 1910, the bicycle race skirted the Pyrenees.

That was a blessing for Greg LeMond, who struggled badly over the sole real climb of the day and lost 18 seconds to his main rivals at the finish. There should have been wild rejoicing in his Z team hotel afterward that "the mountains," such as they were, would not be encountered again for 10 days.

"I'm feeling good but I'm still very tired," the American rider said in a brief chat. Whatever his problem was— fatigue, lost form or illness—it was beginning to show. He also had to struggle on the one climb in the first stage.

So the 255-kilometer (158 miles) Stage Two over fringes of the Pyrenees cannot have been reassuring to LeMond. Imagine if some of the usual peaks had been on the route; but, after leaving San Sebastián, the Tour swung east and picked its way through green valleys while carefully avoiding any giant mountains.

The highest obstacle of the day was the Marie Blanque Pass, at 1,035 meters (3,305 feet) almost a bump in the road. The nearby Tourmalet, for example, rises a majestic 2,115 meters.

At the finish in Pau, after a chilly day through clouds of mist that occasionally turned into rain, the day's honors were shared by Javier Murguialday, a Spaniard with the Amaya team, and Richard Virenque, a Frenchman with RMO. Part of a three-man breakaway that began after 20 kilometers of the stage and reached a peak lead of 22 minutes, they cruised in 5 minutes 5 seconds ahead of the rest of the 195 remaining riders. Murguialday won the stage in 6 hours 41 minutes 56 seconds and Virenque, 3 seconds behind, took the yellow jersey.

That was an arrangement by common courtesy. The Spaniard ranked more than five minutes behind his companion in general classification at the start of the stage and thus could not have gained the overall lead, so each got his prize.

Virenque was in tears after he finished and headed for the victory podium and the yellow jersey. His lead over the second-placed Miguel Indurain was 4:34.

A 22-year-old native of Morocco, Virenque was not considered anywhere near a contender for the final victory.

But who thought that Virenque, with a mere lead of 4 minutes 34 seconds, or seemingly enough time to stroll through Stage Three, would keep the yellow jersey for just one day?

He lost the jersey by less than a country mile—actually about a kilometer—to an RMO teammate, Pascal Lino, but he lost it nevertheless as the race moved from Pau to Bordeaux.

Virenque, who took the symbol of leadership thanks to a long breakaway, was the victim of a similar attack. This time nine riders linked up and went off after 109 kilometers (67 miles) of the 218 flat kilometers (135 miles) from the Pyrenees into Bordeaux wine country.

With the rest of the 195-man field engaged in other pursuits than riding quickly after them, the 9 quickly found themselves with a top lead of more than 15 minutes. At the finish, when Rob Harmeling of the TVM team from the Netherlands won the sprint finish, that lead was reduced to just 6:59.

It was more than enough to put Lino into the yellow jersey. The 25-year-old Frenchman started the day in ninth place overall, trailing Virenque by 5:06.

At exactly 5:07 after he crossed the finish, with Virenque and the rest of the pack still more than a kilometer away, Lino broke into a broad smile and punched his left fist in the air.

"I'm sorry for Richard," he said, somewhat unconvincingly, "but that's racing, isn't it?"

In the general classification, Lino held the yellow jersey by 1:54 over Virenque. Indurain was third, 6:28 behind.

A strong climber who won the Tour of the European Community in 1989 and has won the hill section of the Critérium International, Lino—like his teammate Virenque—was not considered to be a serious challenger for victory when the Tour ended.

But that was what people were saying about Virenque the day before while feeling that he would assuredly wear the yellow jersey until the mountains arrived in a week.

And where was he now? In second place, heartbroken. With Indurain content to ride in the pack and his Banesto team making no effort to control the race, this was becoming a strange Tour de France.

For all its power, Banesto is never a favorite in the team time trial that figures in each Tour de France. That role goes to Panasonic, a pioneer in the discipline, or its Dutch rival Buckler, which best understands the tactics of a team time trial: Riders stay in a tight aerodynamic formation, take turns setting a fast pace at the front and then slip to the rear, making way for the next pacesetter.

Banesto surely had the motors needed—Miguel Indurain himself, Pedro Delgado, Jean-François Bernard, Armand De las Cuevas, Juan Gorospe — but never the coordinated punch. Or perhaps it was part of the same overall strategy that kept Indurain plugging along in the pack and the team indifferent to breakaways. Indurain had announced his plans, hadn't he? His formula was to stay with his rivals in the mountains and crush them in the individual time trials; nothing was said about the first 10 days on the flat or the team time trial.

True to his nature, he seemed not at all upset after the Stage Four time trial, 63.5 kilometers (40 miles) out of and back into Libourne, a wine town near Bordeaux. Before the stage he managed to voice a few fears to satisfy those reporters who needed a story: "I could lose some time," Indurain said, "and if, in the end, the Tour is decided by a few seconds, I don't want to lose it by the time lost here."

Not to worry, he didn't lose much. Banesto finished seventh among the 22 teams, 50 seconds behind the inevitable winner, Panasonic, which clocked one hour 13 minutes 15 seconds on a snaky course during a hot and humid day. Carrera was second, 7 seconds back, followed by Gatorade and Z. Indurain dropped 43 seconds to Claudio Chiappucci, 29 seconds to Gianni Bugno and 10 seconds to Greg LeMond.

Chiappucci professed to be impressed with the results. "The most important thing was to take time on Indurain," the Carrera leader said. "This has been his first defeat in a long time. The best way to beat him is to take time here and there." That was true enough, but why didn't Indurain seem worried?

A Canny Veteran

Stage Five should have been the first of the days of the sprinters, who simply hang on during the climbing and time trials while awaiting their promised land. It is mainly flat, sometimes with a rolling hill or two just far enough from the finish line to allow the sprinters to get to the front and prepare to fight it out.

The 196-kilometer (121-mile) stage from Nogent sur Oise, north of Paris, to Wasquehal, near Belgium, seemed perfect for the sprinters, who yearned to begin using their territory the way Wyatt Earp used the OK Corral.

Instead the 195-man pack again let a big breakaway develop and the first rider to cut a notch in his handlebars was not a young gun but a top sprinter of the 1980s. He was Guido Bontempi, a 32-year-old Italian with the Carrera team, who used to be one of the best in the last 200 meters, where sprinters strut their stuff. He lost that final kick a few years ago and now specializes in the longer path to victory.

Bontempi was part of a 10-man breakaway that developed at kilometer 93 and was allowed its head through the breadbasket of France and its golden fields of wheat ripening in the hot sun.

With five kilometers to the finish and a lead of 3 minutes 47 seconds over the pack, Bontempi bolted off alone from his companions in the breakaway. He won in a total time of 4 hours 6 minutes one second, or 30 seconds better than Dmitri Konichev, a Russian with TVM, and 36 better than Olaf Ludwig, a German with Panasonic.

The pack finished 3:33 later.

In small news about two favorites, Miguel Indurain crashed near the end but quickly remounted, unhurt. Greg LeMond, who had been riding feebly, reported that he was feeling very well and strong now. Smilingly, he said he had finally caught up on his lost sleep.

An Expert's Analysis

What makes a good sprinter?

Davis Phinney, who won two sprint stages in the Tour de France in the late 1980s, was asked that question during the 1992 Tour Du Pont. Phinney rides now only in the United States, for the Coors Light team, but keeps an eye still on races in Europe.

"Genetics, for one, make a sprinter," he replied. "You've got to have it in your muscles. If you don't have a certain amount of explosive power, you can be a good sprinter but not a great one.

"It's fast-twitch fibers that make the difference. As a professional, you've got to go 200, 250 kilometers. Sometimes you call on those fibers and they say, 'No, I don't think so.' They don't often say that to great sprinters."

Phinney continued his analysis:

"Beyond that, you need a certain mentality. You have to be daring, you have to be the kind of guy who doesn't mind mixing it up, who likes to get in there when the race gets to be its craziest."

Max Sciandri of Motorola was not one of these, he said without embarrassment.

"Sometimes I don't do a sprint because it's too dangerous," he admitted. He was talking about field sprints, when the pack comes in together and waves of riders try to get by each other.

"A field sprint is very dangerous," Sciandri said. "I'm really good when there's a hill and the best sprinters drop off and there's a smaller group and I can say something."

To Phinney, Sciandri might be considered a finesse sprinter.

But, Phinney feels, "Finesse sprinting is gone. I don't think you're going to see smaller fast guys dominate sprinting any more. The nature of the business has changed in the last few years. It's a power game and you're talking big bodies out there.

"Now it's the monster power sprinters, the Ludwigs, the Cipollinis, Abdou, the guys who go 300 or 400 meters in the wind, everybody on their wheel, and they just bury everybody."

The funeral ceremony includes rough tactics—bumping an opponent off stride, pulling his jersey to slow him and break his concentration, pushing him with the head or shoulders to make him swerve.

The most common trick is simply for a sprinter to leave his line—move out of his straight path to the finish—to prevent a rival from passing.

Such offenses seemed to have become more common. Djamolidine Abdoujaparov was stripped of his victory over Marion Cipollini in the 1992 Ghent–Wevelgem classic in Belgium because of interference and Wilfried Nelissen of Panasonic was warned publicly about roughness in the Dauphiné Libéré stage race in France.

Phinney knows about roughness, of course. In the Du Pont he was punched in the nose by Michel Zanoli of Motorola just before the sprint.

"There's usually not so much roughness," he said nevertheless. "There are some tricks that everybody knows: how to pen somebody into the fence, how to switch them—when somebody's starting to come around you, you swing two, three feet across the road to knock them back for a second.

"But with sprinters," he continued, "you're going to be with them the next day and maybe you have a big teammate who'll kick some butt.

"There's a hierarchy among sprinters and they don't mess with each other usually, because when you earn your place, you gain a certain amount of respect."

He remembered a race in Italy when, he said, Cipollini pulled on Sean Kelly, the great Irish rider, during a sprint.

"After the race," Phinney said, "all the sprinters crowded around, pointing fingers at Cipollini. He almost caused a riot."

When is the best time to start a sprint?

"Everybody's maximum distance is different," Phinney said. "Three hundred meters is pretty far out there, 400 meters is a bit long because you can't maintain your maximum speed that long." That speed can top 60 kilometers an hour (37 miles an hour).

Rolf Aldag, a German who rode in the Du Pont and was making his debut in the Tour de France for the Helvetia team from Switzerland, offered a few cultural differences between U.S. and European sprinting.

"There's more fighting in Europe because the roads are so narrow," he said. "In the United States, where the roads are so wide, there's no problem in starting your sprint even from 50th place because it's clear ahead.

"Also, Americans are accustomed to the tight turns of a criterium," a city race around and around a short course. "So Americans will begin their sprints around corners. Europeans wait for the straightaway."

Both Phinney and Aldag emphasized the importance of a leadout man, a teammate who sets a fast pace into the final few hundred meters and allows the sprinter to draft on his wheel, saving energy.

"A leadout man is very important in a big group, say 20 men," Aldag said. "Olaf Ludwig is a better sprinter because he rides for Panasonic, which has lots of support.

"If nobody had a leadout, we would all be equal and you might see some different winners." He sighed. His Helvetia team had no strong leadout men.

CHAPTER 6

On the Attack

A frisky Greg LeMond backed up his pronouncements of well-being as he helped power a four-man breakaway on Stage Six that finished one minute 22 seconds ahead of the pack. The performance vaulted him into fifth place in the overall standings.

"I planned to be in the break today," said LeMond, who moved ahead of the defending champion, Miguel Indurain. "I feel a lot stronger." LeMond was 4:29 behind Pascal Lino, the man in the yellow jersey, and 1:04 ahead of Indurain.

LeMond was the last of the four men in the breakaway to splash across the finish line. "I would have liked to win but I'll take the time," he said, jubilant after his show of force for the first time in the race.

The winner was Laurent Jalabert, a Frenchman with the ONCE team, who rode the 167 kilometers (104 miles) from Roubaix, France, to Brussels in 3 hours 37 minutes 6 seconds. Second was Claudio Chiappucci of the Carrera team and third was Brian Holm, a Dane with Tulip.

The stage, run in intermittent rain and under heavy clouds, ended in a drizzle that caused a big crash as the trailing pack passed over slick cobblestones about two miles from the finish. Dozens of riders were hurt, a few seriously.

What had become clear was that no team, not even Indurain's Banesto, was taking responsibility for keeping the race under control and holding breakaways to a minimum. That fit the overall theme of the Tour, which was visiting seven countries to celebrate the beginning of open frontiers and the free movement of people. Free movement was all the Tour had seen so far.

Even the man in the yellow jersey was being allowed to join breakaways. Lino did just that during Stage Seven, 196.5 kilometers (122 miles) from Brussels to Valkenburg, the Netherlands.

Not often was the Tour so bereft of control by one or two of the favorites' teams that the yellow jersey could bound off over the horizon, but that had been the situation since the race started in Spain.

"It's a free race with no one in control," agreed Bernard Hinault, who won the Tour five times, in an interview. "Everybody can attack, anybody can profit.

"There's no boss, nobody in command," explained Hinault, who ran the race with an iron fist on his softer, gentler days.

Lino's escapade did not last to the finish, however. Another breakaway did. When the four lead riders reached Valkenburg after one more gloomy, windy and showery day, Gilles Delion, a Frenchman with the Helvetia team, was the one with his arms aloft.

He finished first in 4 hours 21 minutes 47 seconds. Delion won the stage with a classic move on an uphill finish—he let the three others attack first and then came around them. Neat but not gaudy.

The main pack of riders finished 1:05 behind the winner.

As Hinault said, "It's a dangerous game for Indurain, letting anybody break away." Indurain had been content to ride in the crowd since the race left Spain.

Another five-time winner of the Tour, Eddy Merckx, a Belgian, offered his analysis. "I think that the Giro took a lot out of Indurain's team and they're trying to save energy for the mountains," Merckx said. Although Indurain easily won the Giro d'Italia, his team had to work hard for him.

"Anyway," Merckx added, "everybody is waiting for the time trial in Luxembourg. After that, I think we will have another race." The 65-kilometer (40-mile) race against the clock was two days away.

King of the Walloons

Claude Criquielion realizes that though he may be king of the Walloons, his fellow French-speaking Belgians, he will never become king of Wallonia, their territory. The difference is enormous.

Ask Moreno Argentin, an Italian and the reigning king of Wallonia, a title bestowed by the Liège–Bastogne–Liège bicycle race. Argentin has won it four times since 1985. Criquielion needed to win it only once to ascend to the throne but in 13 years of trying he never finished better than second.

"My fans have been hoping for a long time that I'll win this race," Criquielion admitted. "They're hoping again. Nothing new there."

He was speaking at his hotel before the 77th running of Liège-Bastogne–Liège in 1991. First staged for professionals in 1894, it is the oldest and one of the most distinguished of the classics of the spring season. Twinned with the Flèche Wallonne, which is held four days earlier, Liège Bastogne–Liège is the heart of the sport in the Walloon part of the country.

But no Walloon has won the race since 1978, when Joseph Bruyère did it. Until 1990, in fact, no Belgian had won Liège–Bastogne–Liège since Bruyère. Then Eric Van Lancker, a Dutch-speaker from Flanders, came in an easy first, offering some balm to Belgium, a country scorched by two world wars, haunted by colonial ghosts and everlastingly divided by language. Of the 9.8 million Belgians, nearly 60 percent primarily speak Flemish, a form of Dutch, and 40 percent French.

This balance does not hold in professional bicycling. Few of the great Belgian riders have been Walloons and the current generation abounds with Flemish names: Van Hooydonck, Bruyneel, Museeuw, Vanderaerden, Dhaenens, De Wolf. These Dutch speakers have their own classic, the Tour of Flanders, the northern half of the country; Liège–Bastogne–Liège is for the south. For 13 years Criquielion (Criq or Claudy in the vernacular) was reminded of this every April and for 13 years he tried to oblige.

"I'm in good shape and this is the time of the year that I'm usually at my best," he said before the race. "One more chance."

The finest of the Walloon riders, Criquielion won his share of races, including the Flèche Wallonne twice and the world championship in 1984. (He lost another chance at the title in 1988 when he and Steve Bauer bumped as they led the final sprint and the Belgian crashed.) In 1991, at the age of 34 and in his last season before retirement, Criquielion wore the black, yellow and red jersey of Belgium's champion. When he won the title, he postponed his plan to retire at the end of 1990.

Now, he said, only a victory in the 1991 world championship in Stuttgart could force him to continue for another season. "And I honestly don't expect to win there," he continued. "It's too tough a course for me."

He also did not expect to fulfill his ambition of winning a stage in the Tour de France. A consummate "man of the Tour"— by which the professionals mean a rider who gives full effort, suffers through and completes the world's greatest bicycle race—Criquielion had finished as high as fifth twice without ever winning a stage. He describes this as his greatest disappointment in the sport.

Second, surely, was his failure in Liège–Bastogne–Liège. He came close so many times: seventh in 1984, second in '85, fourth in '86, third in '87.

Three times he was frustrated directly by Argentin. In 1985, Criquielion seemed to have broken away on the race's major hill, the Redoute, but was blocked by a flotilla of photographers' motorcycles just long enough for Stephen Roche, an Irishman, and Argentin to catch up. In the sprint finish, the Italian has few peers and won easily. In 1986, Argentin won a sprint again, this time among six riders, including Criquielion.

Worse was to come in 1987, when Criquielion and Roche broke away but slowly spent the final kilometers watching each other, wondering who was to be first to try to make the decisive move, and forgetting that they were being chased by the pack. With 400 meters remaining, Argentin caught, and beat, them both.

The next three years Argentin was no factor but neither was Criquielion, who finished 26th, 32nd and 14th. Wallonia mourned. "There's a lot of pressure, yes," Criquielion said at his hotel. His thick eyebrows tightened.

Was he confident? "I hope to be at least as good as I was in the Flèche Wallonne." He finished second in that race, beaten by—who else?—Argentin. The Italian had been in splendid form, going on a 70-kilometer (44-mile) breakaway and winning by 2 minutes 20 seconds. Nobody could doubt his strength after he held off all pursuit for such a distance over short and steep hills identical to those in Liège–Bastogne–Liège.

Argentin's message had reached Criquielion. "If I don't win tomorrow," he said, "I hope at least to be in the front."

On the day of the race, Criquielion stayed discreetly in the huge field of riders as they passed the spruce forests of the Ardennes, climbed the first of 10 hills, moved into Bastogne and swung right, on the return leg to Liège, at Patton Tank USA 380152, a memorial to the World War II siege of the town.

A brisk snow began falling as the pack approached the Haussire hill, at 4.6 kilometers the longest of the day. This was familiar territory for Criquielion, who often trained over the hill and who lends his name to a cycling contest there: Beat his best time and win a gold medal. "Everybody here is a fan of his," said Hubert Goffinet, an organizer of the contest. "Criq is the king of the Walloons."

The king and his court of 195 riders were chasing a solitary breakaway, Thierry Bourguinon of the Toshiba team, who was reeled in after 181 kilometers of the 267 in the race. At kilometer 193, with the pack strung out on the Haute Levée hill, Criquielion made his move.

As he accelerated, he kept glancing backward over his left shoulder, wondering who would be able to stay with him. For a few seconds there was nobody and then, suddenly, there was Argentin right on the Belgian's rear wheel. Eight other riders joined them, leaving the pack a minute behind.

The 10 breakaways began to dwindle over the next 70 kilometers and five remaining hills. By the time they reached the Redoute, three hills from home, the group was down to Criquielion, Argentin, his teammate Rolf Sörensen and Miguel Indurain. On the Hornay hill, the next to last, Criquielion tried to speed away but Argentin was right on him, and then so were Sörensen and Indurain.

Sixteen kilometers from the end, on the Forges hill, Criquielion had his last chance to leave the others behind but couldn't. It had been a demanding seven hours and, at age 34, Criquielion was feeling the ride in his legs.

Once over the crest and onto the plain leading into Liège, Argentin and Sörensen, the Ariostea teammates, began playing cat and mouse with the Belgian. Argentin attacked, Criquielion caught him; Sörensen attacked, Criquielion caught him; Sörensen attacked again, Criquielion caught him again. The one time Criquielion attacked, Argentin and Sörensen caught him easily.

"Over the last 30 kilometers I came to terms with the idea that I would lose," Criquielion confessed later. "Against Argentin, all I could do was try to finish second."

The four swept along the Meuse River into Liège and the decisive sprint. With 600 meters to go, Sörensen surged ahead. Criquielion and Argentin were side by side as they passed him and side by side until the final 50 meters, when the Italian displayed his power. He is, after all, one of the sport's best sprinters.

Argentin crossed the line with his arms upraised in victory, coasting as Criquielion still bore down, the length of a bicycle behind.

Minutes later, Criquielion was wiping his dirt-streaked face, removing his helmet and adjusting a clean cloth cap to give his Lotto team maximum publicity before the photographers. Second in the Flèche Wallonne and second in Liège–Bastogne–Liège. He shook his head wearily, the king of the Walloons but not Wallonia.

Happy in the Yellow Jersey

Heading toward the first major shake-out in the Tour de France, Pascal Lino continued to wear the yellow jersey gracefully.

Before Stage Eight began in Valkenburg, the Netherlands, he sat smilingly among a group of Dutch fans eager to photograph him and watch as a masseur rubbed liniment into his legs. Next it was time to provide autographs, give a few interviews and finally sign in for the race. Lino continued to smile throughout.

He was finding, as many have before him, that the yellow jersey has a way of bolstering strength and softening pain.

Vincent Barteau knew just how Lino felt. "One day, two days in the yellow jersey, they're nothing," Barteau said. "A long time, that's everything."

Lino had been leading the race since the third of its 21 stages. With an overall lead of nearly three minutes, Lino was confident he would still be in yellow after the race's first real test, the time trial in Luxembourg.

"I'll lose some time to the favorites but I expect to be among the first 15 finishers," he said. "I think I'll be in the jersey at least until the Alps," which started four days after the time trial.

Certainly he had no problems on Stage Eight, when the pack decided to stick with a bad thing and let another breakaway group of minor riders take all the honors. That made the fourth successive stage over flat or slightly hilly terrain that should have been the sprinters' delight.

Instead, for the fourth successive day, victory went to a relatively obscure rider who escaped from the pack. This time it was Jan Nevens, a Belgian with Lotto.

After a long breakaway with three others, he zipped away from them with a little more than a kilometer to go on the stage, which covered 206.5 kilometers (128 miles) from Valkenburg to Coblenz, Germany, under glowering skies, troublesome winds and occasional rain. One more of the seven frontiers in the Tour was crossed before the race swept by the Moselle and Rhine rivers, passed terraced vineyards and arrived before an enormous crowd in ancient Coblenz.

Nevens finished in 4 hours 45 minutes 23 seconds, or 3 seconds faster than his companions: Jesper Skibby, a Dane with TVM; Massimo Ghirotto, an Italian with Carrera; and Alberto Leanizbarrutia, a Spaniard with Clas.

The main pack among the 184 riders who started the stage finished 4:18 behind Nevens. All the big names—including, for now at least, Lino—were there.

Barteau watched the stage from behind a steering wheel. He retired from professional bicycle racing after the 1990 season and now drove reporters from *l'Équipe*, the French daily sports newspaper and an organizer of the race.

In 1984, Barteau was 22 years old and in his first Tour de France when he was part of a three-man breakaway that finished nearly 20 minutes ahead on the fourth stage. He did not win that stage but took over the yellow jersey on time differential.

"I had 15 minutes' lead," Barteau recalled. "Fifteen is much better than three, like Lino has. He's just like me, a good young rider who climbs OK but not exceptionally."

A Frenchman from Normandy, Barteau was not expected to hold the yellow jersey long, not even into the Pyrenees, which preceded the Alps that year.

"I fooled everybody," Barteau continued. "With the yellow jersey on your back, you can do a lot of things that people don't expect."

He held the jersey, in fact, through the Pyrenees and then surrendered it, exhausted, after the first climb in the Alps. It was the great moment of his career, even better, he said, than when he won every French rider's dream, the Tour de France stage on July 14, the French national holiday.

"That was good too," he said. "Everybody notices." His victory occurred in Marseilles in the 1989 Tour.

The next year he won a stage in the Midi Libre race and, at the finish of the season, retired to operate a fast-food supply network in Normandy. "Restaurants, colleges, clubs—anybody wants fast food, I'll deliver it in my territory."

Each July since then he takes time off to return to the Tour and drive for *l'Équipe.* He said that, at 30, an age when many of his contemporaries are still active, he felt no unhappiness at seeing another Frenchman in the jersey.

"I have no envy," he insisted. "Why should I? I did it and now it's his turn. But he won't hold it as long as I did, 14 days."

Fourteen? The record books and memory said it was 13 days.

"Oh no," Barteau explained. "Fourteen including the rest day," the day off.

"Fourteen," he repeated. "You have to be careful to get these things right. Fourteen."

With an S on His Chest

Anybody wondering where Miguel Indurain had been hiding in the Tour de France got the answer in Luxembourg: He was in a telephone booth changing into a bicycle racing jersey with a very big letter S on it. Absolutely overpowering in a long time trial, Indurain finished more than three minutes ahead of the rest of the 179 remaining riders.

Until the time trial there might have been some doubts about how strong and committed the Spaniard was as he sought his second successive victory in the Tour. No longer.

Riding 65 kilometers (40 miles) out of and back into Luxembourg, Indurain finished in one hour 19 minutes 31 seconds. The second-placed rider, Armand De las Cuevas of Indurain's Banesto team, was a flat three minutes behind.

After that it was sheer destruction. Indurain gained 3:41 on Gianni Bugno, 4:04 on Greg LeMond, 4:12 on Stephen Roche and 5:26 on Claudio Chiappucci, to name his major challengers.

Long minutes after the defending champion finished, came the second big surprise of the day. Pascal Lino, the young Frenchman in the yellow jersey, rode a superb race against the clock and finished fifth, retaining the symbol of leadership.

Overall, Lino was first by 1:27 ahead of Indurain in second place. Third was Jesper Skibby, a nonclimbing Dane with TVM. Roche was fourth and LeMond fifth.

Very rarely does a rider crush his opponents so thoroughly in a long time trial. LeMond lost to Indurain by just eight seconds, for example, in the first time trial in the 1991 Tour.

Excelling at every time check in the race, Indurain rode with his usual fluid grace and power, leaving his main rivals farther behind with each kilometer. Yellow was definitely the color he had in mind as the Tour approached the Alps;

other than Lino, the race had now sorted itself out into the expected battle among the favorites, a group in which Indurain had to rank by far the highest.

Until the time trial, this was not entirely apparent. Since the Tour left Spain, Indurain had done little to defend the No. 1 he wore on his back. LeMond and Chiappucci were especially pesky in the previous week, picking up seconds into Brussels, while Bugno, more careful, had waited for the time trial.

A lot of good it did them. LeMond now stood three minutes behind Indurain overall, Chiappucci 3:27 and Bugno 3:12.

Bugno, who finished second in the last Tour, lost an astonishingly huge eight seconds to Indurain in the first two kilometers of the race against the clock. By seven kilometers, that was up to 22 seconds.

Nor were things going much better for LeMond, who left two minutes after Bugno and four minutes after Indurain. At the seven-kilometer mark, he was five seconds down on the Spaniard.

Since Indurain was ahead of them and his times could be relayed to them, Bugno and LeMond knew what they had to do. Their problem was that they could not stay with the defending champion's pace. By kilometer 37, when the race turned right and headed away from the Moselle River and its traffic of barges and swans, Indurain led Bugno by more than two minutes and LeMond by a bit less.

From then on the Spaniard just kept getting stronger.

When he was about 400 meters from the finish, he caught and passed Laurent Fignon, a Frenchman with Gatorade, and the huge and noisy crowd gasped. In a time trial, the riders leave separately, in reverse order of standing, and Fignon had started six minutes before Indurain.

Lino did almost as well, catching his two-minute man, Jens Heppner, a German with Telekom, who was in second place before the start. He dropped to seventh.

116

In reality, it was a fine time trial for almost all the top-ranked riders, who finished near each other. For Indurain it was a superb time trial.

The course—mainly flat and straight except for a small climb and some gentle curves—called for little technical ability. What was demanded was strength, which Indurain had in abundance. As usual, he rode with a look of unemotional determination, not even grimacing slightly when he left the paved highway and bumped onto cobblestones in the village of Ehnen, halfway through the course.

All sorts of equipment was in evidence for the time trial as riders varied their wheels, frames, saddles and handlebars, seeking an extra advantage. Most riders used a rear disc wheel but from then on it was anybody's choice.

The most cutting-edge rider was Chiappucci, who lost the decisive time trial to LeMond in the 1990 Tour when the Italian showed up with a standard road bicycle. This time he had a natty aerodynamic helmet, aerodynamic bars, a disc wheel, power shifting and everything else except a horn and a kick stand.

For all the good the gadgets did him against Indurain, Chiappucci should have added a motor.

Hard Times for Buckler

Only a year before, by the time the Tour de France approached the mountains after the usual first 10 days on the plains, the Buckler team would have registered a victory or two and been close in other stages.

No more. Plagued by the same economic uncertainty that affected nearly a third of the 22 teams in the Tour de France, Buckler had not come close to a victory.

Although team officials denied it, a long difficulty in finding a new sponsor in a time of recession and multiple other rivals for sports advertising dollars had cost Buckler its sense of teamwork. Now riders for the Dutch team were all looking for jobs for the next season. In that situation, a rider will not gladly discard his chances of impressing a prospective employer just for the sake of helping his leader, his sprinter or even his team.

The concept of sacrifice, so essential in professional bicycle racing, did not make it down to the bottom line.

That was proven when the Tour tackled the tenth stage, 217 kilometers (135 miles) of rolling countryside from Luxembourg to Strasbourg, France.

In the first mass sprint finish since the race started, Jean-Paul van Poppel, a Dutchman with PDM, just beat Djamolidine Abdoujaparov, an Uzbek with Carrera. Laurent Jalabert, a Frenchman with ONCE, was third—scant consolation on July 14, the French national day.

Almost all the pack finished in the same time as the winner, 5 hours 2 minutes 45 seconds, and Pascal Lino of RMO remained in the yellow jersey of the overall leader. He was 1:27 ahead of Miguel Indurain, whose extraordinary performance in the previous day's time trial remained the major topic of conversation before the stage.

"I've never seen a rider dominate a Tour de France field like that," said Bernard Thévenet, who won the Tour twice in the mid-1970s. "Three minutes ahead of everybody else is unbelievable."

Now that he was on the road to a second consecutive victory, Indurain's Banesto team, with the help of ONCE, began to keep the race under control, chasing down the few breakaways and thus setting up the field sprint.

Of Indurain's challengers, the most active one was Gianni Bugno, in sixth place overall. He twice tried to power breakaways before the race finished in Alsace, passing adjacent fields of hops and barley in the beer basket, or perhaps barrel, of France.

The results were not cheering to Buckler, whose highest finisher was Eric Vanderaerden, ninth in the sprint. That was not the way to attract new financing.

The Dutch team was just one among many facing the loss of a sponsor. Others included Greg LeMond's Z, RMO, PDM, Panasonic, Helvetia and Tulip, all among the big names in professional bicycling. Of those, only Panasonic was reported to be ready to sign a new contract, but a news conference to announce the agreement, scheduled later in the week, was suddenly postponed.

Even RMO, which was basking in the publicity glare of Lino's yellow jersey, was pessimistic about the next season. The main sponsor, a temporary employment agency, said that it could not continue without some budgetary partners.

In a series of interviews, the others reported that in the dismal international economic situation, prospective sponsors were wary of committing themselves to team budgets that often exceed $5 million annually.

"We're optimistic, we're hopeful, but it's a lot of money and sponsors don't want to spend it right now," said Roger Legeay, the directeur sportif of the Z team.

Bernard Vallet, who coached the Toshiba team from France that folded in 1991, put some numbers to this picture.

"I talked to 400 prospective sponsors in 6 months last year and not a one was finally willing to sign up," Vallet said. "Too much money for them or they had other commitments."

In a year heavy with major sports competition, these other commitments included the Olympic Games in Barcelona and the European Soccer Championships in Sweden.

"The people I talked with were signed up for other sports for the next few years," Vallet said. He was attending the Tour as a driver for an apricot-growing cooperative that was advertising its fruit in the publicity caravan that precedes the race.

"It's much cheaper than sponsoring a team," Vallet noted. "Plus the publicity caravan never loses."

Winning results alone do not attract or keep a sponsor, however.

Roger Zannier, who had sponsored the Z team for six seasons, planned to withdraw at the end of the Tour, win or lose, he said.

"I've been saying that for a year," he continued. "The Z team has been very good for business but it's time to try something else."

Z is his trademark for mass-market children's clothing in Europe. Since the team took the name and especially since LeMond won the 1989 Tour on the last stage in Paris, the publicity value had been remarkable.

The Buckler team had known for three years, since it signed its sponsor, a maker of nonalcoholic beer, that the company would retire at the end of 1992.

For the last year, Harrie Jansen, the Buckler team's manager, had traveled the world to find another backer. "America, Japan, all over Europe," Jansen said. "It's very difficult." He remained hopeful, he insisted, despite the obstacles.

He listed the usual reasons: the global recession and the Summer Olympics and soccer championships. To them he added the Winter Olympics in Albertville, France, and the International Exposition in Seville, Spain.

In the United States, where he had met with companies he declined to name, he pointed out a particular problem: the growth of event, rather than team, sponsorship.

"An event is a rather sure exposure," he said. "Investing in a team is a much more dynamic course but it's not so sure that you'll get a result. Teams lose as well as win."

Buckler had more often won. In the computerized standings, it ranked fourth among the 22 teams in the Tour and was feared especially in the classics.

But it was expensive.

Jansen recalled cheaper times, like 1984. That was just before the boom in rider salaries that started at the end of that season when LeMond signed a million-dollar contract, probably tripling the top scale.

"The budget now is out of control," Jansen judged. "Five or six million dollars is more than most sponsors can afford. We have to cut that in half by reducing salaries, cutting back to 14 riders from 18 or 20, losing some technical help. Nobody will pay this sort of money now."

He was also critical of the Tour de France for signing as major sponsors the Crédit Lyonnais bank, Coca Cola and the Fiat auto makers.

"So they get exclusive rights to publicity" in the caravan that precedes the Tour, he noted. "Indurain's Banesto team is sponsored by a bank and it cannot appear in the caravan with more than one vehicle.

"Therefore you can rule out as sponsors all banks, all soft-drink companies and all car companies," Jansen continued. "The Tour, the greatest bicycle race, is helping to kill the sport."

Back in the Broom Wagon

At 11:47 A.M., a short while after the start of Stage 11, Roberto Sierra decided that the pain in his left thigh was too intense, the road ahead too steep and long and the rest of the field in the Tour de France too far ahead to be overtaken by him.

Sierra, a 25-year-old Spaniard who rode for the Clas team, pulled over to the right and got off his bicycle, which a mechanic began attaching to the roof of a team car.

In moments, Raymond Guilmin, a race official, had bustled from a red van and began removing two placards with Sierra's race number, 168, from the back of the rider's shorts. Guilmin looked moderately unhappy and made sure he patted Sierra on the shoulder when he was done.

Then Guilmin directed the Spaniard toward the van. In French it is called the *voiture balai*, literally the broom wagon, and it is used to sweep up riders who quit the Tour de France.

Sierra climbed in as the van's driver, Jacques Lauret, cautioned him to watch his head. Crying quietly and looking stunned at his showing in his first Tour de France, Sierra spent the next five hours in the van, following the Tour at its very tail and listening to details of the daily stage on the radio. It links all Tour vehicles, including reporters' and even the *voiture balai.*

Not that Sierra was interested as he sat initially with his dark face hidden in his hands. OK? he was asked in the universal language since none of the others spoke acceptable Spanish.

"Bueno," he said. Then he rubbed his hand along his left thigh. "Impossible," he added with a Spanish pronunciation.

He reported, too, that he did not speak or follow French well, and that is the language of Radio Tour.

So he missed nearly all the news: How Miguel Indurain, Pascal Lino, Gianni Bugno and Claudio Chiappucci joined an early breakaway on the 249.5-kilometer (155-mile) stage from Strasbourg to Mulhouse in the east of France.

How Greg LeMond had "extreme difficulty," as the radio put it, in the first climbs and fell more than two minutes behind the other favorites at the 100-kilometer mark.

How, with the help of his Z team, LeMond eventually got back to the Indurain group and how Laurent Fignon, the winner of the 1983 and 1984 Tours and the man LeMond beat by 8 seconds in the 1989 Tour, won the stage. The Frenchman finished in 6 hours 30 minutes 49 seconds after escaping before the last of seven climbs in the Vosges Mountains and its foothills.

Second, 12 seconds behind Fignon, was Laurent Dufaux, a Swiss who rode for Helvetia. It was Fignon's ninth stage victory in the Tour and the first in many years.

The favorites all finished 22 seconds back and there was no major change in the overall standings as the Tour arrived at its only day off in the three weeks it would take to move from San Sebastián to the Champs-Élysées.

Guilmin and Lauret did not hear much of this either as they rode in the front seats of the *voiture balai*. It has 15 other seats but one was taken up by their luggage and another by a reporter, leaving the ominous number of 13 for riders who could go no farther.

The reason Guilmin and Lauret did not pay attention to breakaways, recoveries and other successes is that they occupy themselves only with failure.

When Rolf Golz, a German with Ariostea, took off from almost the first kilometer and built an instant and huge lead, Guilmin and Lauret showed no reaction. When Radio Tour announced, however, that rider No. 41 needed medical attention as he rolled along, they exchanged quick glances.

A rider seeking a doctor is often not far removed from a rider dropping out of the race, and Guilmin looked around the van to check on its readiness. There were five open boxes of soft drinks, 24 small cans to the box, and a blanket. Next to the two men in the front seat was an ice chest with fruit and drinks. A plastic bag full of pastries dangled from a knob on the dashboard. There was an old champagne box for rubbish.

And a broom lay on the floor under the two-seat benches that ran down the right side, looking back from the driver.

"That's just to sweep the van out," Lauret said. "We don't put a broom outside any more." Either aloft over the front or rear windows or hanging below the front bumper, the broom had been the symbol of the *voiture balai* since it was introduced decades ago.

"No more," Lauret continued. "Those were our instructions."

Guilmin tried to explain. "I think they thought it was too old-fashioned," he said. "You've got to keep up with the times."

He was 71 years old and in his 21st Tour as a commissaire, or international bicycling official, including the last 6 in the van. Before that he worked from a motorcycle.

Lauret, 62 and, like Guilmin, a Frenchman, had been driving the van for 12 years.

Both are kind and patient men, and they made certain that Sierra was comfortable before they resumed driving.

Traveling far back, the van has a limited view of the Tour: just ahead of it is a flatbed truck that picks up riders' bicycles when they quit, just behind it a flatbed truck that picks up cars when they crash. Behind the second flatbed truck was a blue van marked "fin de course," or end of the race.

Only when the Tour swings left or right through a long curve do the two men get a glimpse of the real race, and then it is only of team cars bearing more bicycles. So far back is the van that it passed a sign warning that the first climb was a kilometer ahead just as Radio Tour announced the results of that climb.

When the two men see a rider, he is always in trouble. Somebody like Jean-Claude Leclercq, a Frenchman with the Helvetia team, who was pedaling slowly through the Alsatian town of Ste. Marie aux Mines, far behind the pack.

The van stayed close behind Leclercq for many kilometers as the two men awaited his surrender. There was obviously too much distance for a single rider to make up on the 177-man pack, which was traveling far faster than any one man could do.

Even if he finished, Leclercq faced certain elimination on time differential with the winner and the Frenchman was enough of a veteran to have figured this out.

"He'll probably quit at the feed zone," Guilmin judged. The *voiture balai* pulled over to an ambulance, which, with a motorcycle policeman, was sandwiching the rider.

"How far can he go?" Guilmin asked a nurse in the front seat of the ambulance. The first of two feed zones was 14 kilometers ahead. The nurse said she thought Leclercq could make it. Slowly he began climbing toward the Bagenelles Pass, rated second category out of five for toughness, length and steepness.

As Leclercq pedaled doggedly on, Guilmin watched to make sure he did not solicit pushes from the thousands of fans along the way. That is illegal and brings a fine in money and time.

At the feed zone, where the rest of the pack had long before grabbed bags of sandwiches, fruit and pastries, a Helvetia car was waiting on the left. Leclercq drifted over to it, dismounted and greeted the broom wagon.

Lauret reached out his window and removed the two placards, No. 76, and passed them to Guilmin. Both men sighed.

Unlike Sierra, Leclercq was allowed to get into his team car because it was used for the feeding and was not part of the proper race. To prevent fraud, it is illegal for a rider to quit and enter his team's first two cars, which travel behind the pack.

Then the *voiture balai* moved off again, looking for more trouble. Ten minutes later, Francis Moreau, a Frenchman with the GB-MG team, was spotted, struggling and far behind the pack before a big climb.

The van moved into position.

By the end of the stage, Guilmin had collected five sets of numbers on what was really an undemanding stage in the mountains. The Alps were still two days away.

No Rest for the Weary

The Tour tightened dramatically at the top during Stage 12 as two former winners of the race moved close to the yellow jersey. They were Stephen Roche and Pedro Delgado, who had each won the Tour once and were relegated now to a lieutenant's role on their teams. Another former winner, Greg LeMond, struggled again on the climbs and conceded that his hopes of overall victory were flimsy.

"Victory?" LeMond repeated in an interview. "Not unless I can turn myself around 100 percent in the next day or two."

He was asked how he hoped to do that. "I don't know," he said slowly. "I just don't know."

LeMond did not find out during the 12th and longest stage of the Tour. Leaving Dole and arriving in St. Gervais just outside the highest Alps, the race covered 267.5 kilometers (166 miles) under a hot sun.

At the finish, 7 hours 10 minutes 56 seconds after the start, the winner was Rolf Jaermann, a Swiss with the Ariostea team and no factor in the overall contest. Right behind him were two big, and slightly unexpected, factors. Delgado, a Spaniard with Miguel Indurain's Banesto team, was three seconds back. Roche, an Irishman with Claudio Chiappucci's Carrera team, was 39 seconds behind Jaermann.

The pack, including such riders as Pascal Lino, Indurain, Chiappucci, Gianni Bugno and LeMond crossed the line 2:56 behind the winner.

That worked out to Roche's staying in third place overall behind Lino and Indurain but closing the gap to 1:58. Delgado moved from ninth place to fourth, 4:08 back, and LeMond dropped a button to fifth, 4:27 behind.

The American insisted that his morale was not suffering.

"My morale is actually pretty good,' he said. "It's just that..." and he paused for a deep sigh, "I can't understand why..."

One reason, he thought, was the extremely fast pace of the 79th Tour. The stage to St. Gervais averaged more than 37 kilometers an hour (23 mph), exceptionally rapid with five climbs on the menu.

"It's been extremely hard," LeMond said. "We haven't had any days where we've just rolled along to recuperate.

"It's been the world championship or a classic every day," he said. "Each day I think everybody is going to tire out today and go slow, and it hasn't happened yet. Today it won't, tomorrow it won't." The race was going into the highest Alps for the weekend.

"But I haven't given up," LeMond said, suddenly sounding lively. "I never give up.

"I'm being realistic too. Indurain is riding unbelievably well."

Front and Center

The big boys, the strong men, the Miguel Indurains, Claudio Chiappuccis and Gianni Bugnos, took over the Tour as it spent the first of two destructive days in the high Alps. Nearly everybody else was swept away, including Greg LeMond, who finished nearly 50 minutes back after fading badly in the early climbing, and Pascal Lino, who had worn the yellow jersey for a week and a half.

At the end of Stage 13, Indurain was back in a familiar position—first in general classification. Chiappucci, the winner of the stage, was second, 1:42 behind the Spaniard, and Bugno was third, 4:20 back.

The stage, from St. Gervais to Sestriere, Italy, covered 254.5 kilometers (158 miles) and Chiappucci rode the bravest race of his career to win it. The Italian, who yearns for recognition, gathered it by the ton. He set off with nine companions on the second of five major climbs, shed them one by one and continued alone over the top of the third climb and for the rest of the afternoon.

In all, he rode without a relay—which would have given him a chance to save some energy— for nearly four hours under a sun so hot that Chiappucci could smell the melted tar on the road as he neared the finish line. He also had to pedal through a scandalously unruly crowd of Italian fans, who ran alongside him, screaming encouragement, dousing him with water, making him swerve and patting and slapping him as he passed. With a kilometer to go and Indurain riding like a machine more than a minute behind him, Chiappucci finally shook a fist at his tormentors.

And then he was glancing back, seeing nobody there, and pumping his right fist in the air, home free.

Chiappucci was clocked in 7 hours 44 minutes 51 seconds. Second was Franco Vona of Italy and the GB-MG team, 1:34 behind. Indurain surprisingly faded in the final kilometer and finished third, 1:45 behind, with Bugno fourth, 2:53 behind, and Andy Hampsten of Motorola fifth, 3:27 behind. The fragmented pack began arriving nearly six minutes after Chiappucci, and Lino was 10:33 down, which dropped him from first place to fourth. It was a hard day.

First came the Saisies Pass, 1,533 meters (5,388 feet) high and, rated second category, the easiest of the day's five climbs. As it mounted, the road passed thick stands of spruce trees and high pastures ringing with the sound of cow bells. Then came a long sinuous descent to the valley floor, which led only to the next climb.

To the sound of a brass band, including flugelhorns, in the village of Beaufort, the pack began to climb toward the 1,968-meter-high Cormet de Roselend, rated first class. Le-Mond began to lose ground there, and Chiappucci to gain it.

Then it was back to the valley floor at Bourg St. Maurice for the first of two feed zones before the road began again to mount. A sign terrifying in its implications to the strung-out pack announced that the next summit was 37 kilometers, all of them uphill, away. This was the Iseran Pass, rated beyond category at 2,770 meters. The ascent did not turn really nasty until the last 11 kilometers, where Chiappucci was becoming a solitary rider for the rest of the afternoon.

The tree line gave out long before the top, even long before the first patches of snow appeared. Chiappucci sped over the Mont Cenis Pass, first category at 1,746 meters, and into Italy for the final climb. That was a 32-kilometer-long ramp to Sestriere, 2,020 meters high and first category again. Indurain, Vona, Bugno and Hampsten were all together in the chase, but Chiappucci held them off easily.

He was beaming at the finish, knowing that the last man to win a Tour stage into Sestriere, decades before, had also been an Italian—the immortal Fausto Coppi. That was the sort of company Chiappucci felt he belonged in.

CHAPTER 7

Making the Headlines

Americans made the news, good and bad, at Alpe d'Huez as Andy Hampsten easily won the climbers' crown jewel and Greg LeMond dropped out of the race he had won three times.

"It's such a terrific feeling," Hampsten said after he crossed the line. "For me, it's the world championship to win a stage like this before half a million people.

"Whenever people back home ask about Alpe d'Huez, I always tell them that other mountains are more difficult to climb but there's nothing like this place for prestige."

Some of those half-million fans on the final sun-baked mountain did their best to share in his triumph. Running beside him and screaming encouragement, standing in his path and drenching him with water, they finally got to Hampsten. Normally even-tempered, he slapped aside a fan's bottle of water with three kilometers to go and then swiped at a boy who nearly blocked his way. Near the end Hampsten was riding through a sea of spectators that parted for him only at the last moment.

Crowd control was not a strength in the 79th Tour.

Hampsten, who rode for Motorola and had finished as high as fourth in previous Tours without winning a stage, jumped away from his companions in a five-man break-away to win by more than a minute. This followed his fifth place in the previous day's stage in the high Alps, which took a dreadful toll of the field.

Among the most illustrious victims was LeMond. Suffering from pain in his right knee and general exhaustion, he made it over only one of the three formidable climbs before he quit. The pack was far ahead and the only company LeMond had on the road was his teammate,

Gilbert Duclos-Lassalle, who had done his best to try to pace his leader. But they were so far behind that they realized they would be eliminated from the Tour on time differential. When he coasted into the feed zone and got off his bicycle and into a team car, LeMond was half an hour behind the front of the pack. He started the stage in 41st place after losing 49 minutes 38 seconds on the previous day's climb to Sestriere, Italy.

So ended his dream of again wearing the leader's yellow jersey he took home after the Tours of 1986, 1989 and 1990.

Hampsten, who is a year younger than LeMond and has long been known as "the other American," had power enough for two. He finished the 186.5-kilometer (115-mile) stage from Sestriere to Alpe d'Huez in 5 hours 41 minutes 58 seconds and in full command when it counted, up the 21 hairpin turns to the French resort.

Second for the second successive day was Franco Vona, an Italian with GB-MG, 1:17 behind. Third, 2:08 back, was Eric Boyer, a Frenchman with LeMond's Z team.

"Eric's our leader now," said Michel Laurent, the Z manager. "He's our boy and he's all we've got left." Boyer did not rank in the top 10 overall.

With his victory and fifth place the previous day, Hampsten jumped from 21st place to eighth to third, 8:01 behind Miguel Indurain. Hampsten was not a top-echelon time trialer and, with an eight-minute deficit, could not realistically be expected to be a candidate for overall victory.

"I'm not waiting for the time trial to try to do something," joked Hampsten, who also predicted that "next week is going to be ugly for a lot of riders." He meant that the competition for the final victory podium would turn fierce.

The man that ugliness would primarily be aimed at was Indurain, who finished a strong sixth on the way to Alpe d'Huez and solidified his lead over all but the most pesky challenger. That would be Claudio Chiappucci, who finished fifth, a bicycle length ahead of Indurain, and remained in second place overall, 1:42 behind.

Chiappucci is another middling time trialer but brims over with energy and was ready and willing to attack anywhere and several times a day, if need be.

What was expected to be the showdown time trial was scheduled five days off in the Loire Valley of France. There were four stages before that where a man of Chiappucci's zest and low cunning could hope to spring an ambush.

No other rider was left in the race to stop Indurain from winning for the second successive year, accident or sickness permitting. Such possible challengers as Gianni Bugno, Stephen Roche, Pedro Delgado and Luc Leblanc were all left far back in the dust as the major climbing started and ended.

Indurain went for the early knockout on the way to Alpe d'Huez, attacking with a teammate on flat terrain after a small first climb, the Montgenèvre Pass, rated second category in length, steepness and toughness. Or perhaps Big Mig was simply testing his challengers' alertness and will power, not to say legs. They reeled him in quickly on a wonderfully sunny day that washed the Alps and their glaciers in light and, after many days of dark clouds, wind and rain, made the world seem new.

The Galibier Pass, 2,640 meters (8,712 feet) high and rated beyond category in difficulty, came next. After that was the Croix de Fer Pass, 2,067 meters high and beyond category.

Finally came Alpe d'Huez, 1,460 meters high, beyond category and often beyond comprehension with its vast ocean of spectators and its riders struggling ever upward through them, striving for victory.

As Hampsten put it, "For a climber, there's nothing like this."

The Morning After

Looking freshly shaved and showered, Luc Leblanc left his hotel atop Alpe d'Huez before breakfast and started to cross the Place Jean Moulin to buy a newspaper. On his way, he paused to look out across the Alps and simply shook his head slowly from side to side.

Many other riders who started the Tour de France knew that feeling.

Until the weekend, Leblanc, a 25-year-old Frenchman and team leader for Castorama, ranked as an outside choice to finish in the top three.

His hopes ended, however, in the high Alps. After finishing 49 minutes, 38 seconds behind on the Italian stage, he was so far back on the way to Alpe d'Huez that he was eliminated on time differential with the winner, Andy Hampsten. Leblanc had some medical excuses, including knee problems. What he was really a victim of was the race's extraordinarily fast pace. The Tour was averaging 39.5 kilometers an hour (24.5 mph). If maintained to Paris, that would have made this the fastest Tour de France since the race began in 1903.

Mountain stages barely dragged down the average. Climbing over three alpine peaks rated beyond category in toughness, length and steepness, for example, Hampsten finished in an average speed of an astounding 37.7 kilometers an hour.

Further, when Leblanc, and Greg LeMond too, finished in a large group of riders 49:38 behind into Sestriere, they all matched the fastest time for a winner predicted for the stage by the Tour's own guide. On that stage from St. Gervais, France, three riders were eliminated on time differential, 14 quit and one did not start. From Sestriere to Alpe d'Huez, three more including Leblanc were outside the time limit; eight, including LeMond, quit and one was disqualified. That left the original field of 198 riders reduced to 133, or the fewest since 1986, when 132 men finished what 210 started.

And there were still six stages to go.

Although the high Alps were far behind now, the pace was not slowing. That was shown on Stage 15, a 198-kilometer (123-mile) jaunt from Bourg d'Oisans past fruit orchards and cornfields to the grimy city of St. Étienne.

Finishing nearly half an hour ahead of the fastest time predicted in the Tour guide, Franco Chioccioli of the GB-MG team was an easy winner after a shortish breakaway. Chioccioli came across the line in 4 hours 43 minutes 59 seconds, or 42 seconds ahead of Dmitri Konichev of TVM and 43 seconds ahead of Giancarlo Perini of Carrera.

The leaders' pack finished 6 seconds behind Perini and there were no major changes in the overall standings.

The winner, Chioccioli, had something to celebrate beside the stage: Back home in Italy, his wife gave birth to their first child, a son, the day before. He also had a small problem. Before the start, Chioccioli told friends he would name his son after the stage winner. Call the boy Junior.

Chioccioli, who won the Giro d'Italia two years before and finished third in 1992, is the GB-MG team leader and one of the few leaders, other than Miguel Indurain of Banesto, who could finish this race with unchallenged status.

By the start of the 15th stage, 8 of the 22 teams had lost their leaders to the many challenges. Those ousted included Leblanc, LeMond of Z, Charly Mottet of RMO, Federico Echave of Clas, Moreno Argentin of Ariostea and Laudelino Cubino of Amaya—all stars of the sport.

"It's easier for a leader to drop out than it is for an ordinary rider," Leblanc told l'Équipe. "A leader doesn't want to look ridiculous. You have to know how to keep your dignity."

That was open to debate, but not his next remark.

"In cycling," Leblanc thought, "when you're going badly, you're all alone."

More Changes of Plans

The directeur sportif of Greg LeMond's Z team confirmed officially the next morning that the American would not attempt to break the world record for the hour's bicycle ride against the clock a month after the Tour ended.

The attempt, planned for more than a year, was contingent on LeMond's form and spirit after the Tour de France and became the first consequence of his withdrawal because of exhaustion and a painful right knee.

Or was it the first? Some people were asking now if LeMond's illustrious career was also not imperiled and near its finish.

Was he finished in the one race that means the most to him? Was he finished, at 31, in the sport of professional bicycle racing itself?

LeMond denied this strongly. "This just shows how hard the Tour is," he insisted. "It's not the end of an era."

Others were not so sure.

"I don't know about finished but he's certainly closer to the finish than he was at the start of the Tour," said Vincent Barteau, a former teammate of LeMond's and a close friend. "Having to quit like that really does something to your morale, something bad."

"We'll see, we can't tell yet if he's finished," said Bernard Hinault, who won the Tour five times. Like Barteau, he is a Frenchman and a former teammate of LeMond's but not a friend. The two battled it out for the victory in 1986 although Hinault had publicly promised to help his protege win.

"What we do know is that LeMond's taken a very hard blow to his morale and without strong morale, you're finished."

Bernard Thévenet, who won the Tour twice in the mid-1970s, placed similar emphasis on morale.

"What LeMond needs is an exploit, maybe at the world championships, a real exploit to lift his morale," Thévenet said. "If he can accomplish that, it will be much easier to come back strong next year."

Thévenet spoke before the start of Stage 16, which covered 212 kilometers (131 miles) from St. Étienne to La Bourboule, a thermal resort noted for its arsenic-laden waters. They are said to cure many ills, perhaps quickly.

The stage was won by Stephen Roche, the Irishman who rode for Carrera and finished first in the 1987 Tour before going into a decline himself. Starting in hot and sunny weather, he arrived in cold fog and drizzle in a countryside littered with dormant volcanoes. Roche's time was 5 hours 53 minutes 14 seconds, with Slava Ekimov of Panasaonic second, 46 seconds back, and Jon Unzaga of Clas third, 50 seconds back.

The leaders' pack arrived just after Unzaga and there were no changes at the top, where Miguel Indurain remained in the yellow jersey and Claudio Chiappucci 1:42 behind him.

Indurain's domination of the 79th Tour had been constant and his bright future was a major factor in LeMond's.

"What's certain is that there are riders, like Indurain, who are younger than Greg," said Roger Legeay, LeMond's directeur sportif. In confirming that the attempt on the hour record had been scratched, Legeay was somewhat cryptic when he discussed his star.

"I can't believe that a rider of his quality is finished at 31," said Legeay, a former rider himself and the man who recruited LeMond for the Z team in 1989.

What causes a rider to decline?

"It's much more a drop in motivation than in your legs," Thévenet answered.

Graham Jones, an Englishman and a former rider for French and English teams from 1979 to 1988, was less sure.

"I don't think a rider ever does realize really why and how he's in decline," Jones said. "There's always hope that it will come back. But I think one day you have to make the decision that you're not going to do it and just retire, as I did.

"I decided the time had come when I thought I wasn't doing justice to myself."

Jones also thought LeMond was not through. "Nope, definitely not," he said. "He's still not old by cycling standards and I think he can come back."

John Eustice, a former American rider in Europe and at home until he retired in 1990, was also unsure why an athlete declines.

"I think you never really know why you're declining," said Eustice, who was conducting Tour interviews for the ESPN cable television station. "And even if you know, you don't want to know.

"What happens is you have a lot of strength but there come certain points where you just don't have it," he continued. "When the others go a higher speed, when there's that little extra thing you can't do—when those little things start happening, they add up.

"And you can't explain why you don't have it and you think, 'Well that must have been a problem, it's going to be O.K.'

"It's very hard to be reasonable, especially for champions like LeMond because they're unreasonable and that's why they're champions."

Eustice then repeated a remark that Indurain, three years younger than LeMond, made during an interview: "Greg will have to learn to accept the laws of life, just as I will have to learn to accept them some day."

Hampsten's Turnaround

Dreaming about a place on the victory podium when the Tour de France ended, Andy Hampsten nevertheless insisted that he was treating the world's greatest bicycle race as anything but.

"I no longer look on the Tour as the only race," he said. "I no longer feel that if I don't do well here, my season's been a failure. That pressure is off.

"So now it's just another race."

The American began grappling with this insight two years before. Only after his victory in the big climbing stage at Alpe d'Huez did he feel he had it in a hammerlock.

"It took a while," he admitted. He also credited his physical maturity at the age of 30, a new sense of relaxation and confidence plus a winter spent in Europe, instead of Boulder, Colorado, in heavy duty training.

They all added up to a changed rider in the Tour, where he had never finished better than fourth. That was far below his victories in the Giro d'Italia in 1988 and in the Tour of Switzerland in 1986 and 1987.

Hampsten was a 24-year-old rider in his second year as a professional when he finished fourth in the 1986 Tour. He did worse the next three years: 16th in 1987, 15th in 1988 and 22d in 1989. In 1990, when he began trying to relax and not overestimate the Tour, he finished 11th. In 1991 he was eighth and now he ranked third overall.

The Motorola rider easily held that spot as the 131 remaining riders completed a farcical 189-kilometer (117-mile) jaunt over rolling countryside from La Bourboule to Montluçon in the center of France.

The winner of Stage 17 was Jean-Claude Colotti, a Frenchman with the Z team, who finished in 4 hours 34 minutes 55 seconds or 3:31 ahead of the next two riders and 16:15 ahead of the main pack.

Colotti was part of a three-man breakaway with two riders for Dutch teams, Marc Sergeant of Panasonic and Frans Maassen of Buckler. The highest ranked of them, Sergeant, was in 80th place overall, more than 2 hours 14 minutes behind, before the stage. So the pack let them go, knowing they were no threat to the overall standings.

But the two Dutch teams are dreadful rivals and Sergeant and Maassen spent so much time watching each other and refusing to work for the common good that Colotti was able to dash away unheeded 34 kilometers from the line. For most of the rest of that distance, Sergeant and Maassen continued to survey each other.

Maassen finally came in second and Sergeant third, when a bit of cooperation could have given either the victory. Try explaining that to them.

Miguel Indurain continued untroubled in the overall leader's yellow jersey, 1:42 ahead of Claudio Chiappucci, with Hampsten third, 8:07 behind. Colotti's average speed was a rapid 41.2 kilometers an hour (25.4 mph).

The day that would decide whether Hampsten was one of the three riders to mount the podium on the Champs-Élysées was two stages away. A 64-kilometer time trial was on the calendar then and Hampsten is just a middling rider in the race against the clock.

CHAPTER 8

Rubbing It In

The Loire Valley proved to be another killing ground for Miguel Indurain.

On Stage 18, 212 kilometers (131 miles) over flat and picturesque country from Montluçon to Tours, the defending champion sat in the pack as Thierry Marie, a Frenchman with Castorama, won only the second field sprint of the Tour, edging the few other sprinters who survived the Alps. Jelle Nijdam, a Dutchman with Buckler, was second and Johan Museeuw, a Belgian with Lotto, was third.

Marie finished in 5 hours 7 minutes 15 seconds, the same time as nearly everybody else. Once again the pace was high: 41.3 kilometers an hour (26 mph). The pack stayed mostly together as it passed such eyefuls as the renaissance fortress in Culan, the equally old chateau in Montrésor and hundreds of fields of stunted sunflowers finally catching some rays after weeks of rain.

Indurain maintained his lead and then, the next day, rode away from nearly everybody again in the final time trial and more than doubled his lead with two days to go. The one rider who resisted, Gianni Bugno, awoke from a long sleep to take over third place from Andy Hampsten. Bugno was the only man not to finish nearly two and a half minutes back.

He crossed the line 40 seconds slower than the defending champion. Indurain lengthened his leadership to 4 minutes 35 seconds from the 1:42 it was before the stage.

"It's nice to win stages, but my goal is to win the Tour de France," Indurain said afterward in careful tones. Barring catastrophe, he was certain to mount the final victory podium.

Hampsten would not. The American dropped into fourth place and the podium holds only the top three.

Still, as he likes to say, there is always a winner in a bicycle race but there are never losers since 129 out of 130 men cannot be considered losers.

Hampsten was followed in his Motorola team car by his great friend and idol, Eddy Merckx, the Belgian who won the Tour de France five times two decades ago. Although Merckx came for the day from Belgium to lend inspiration, encouragement and advice, they were not enough. Hampsten started strong but slackened long before the end. The victory podium would have to remain simply a goal.

The others who would almost certainly be up there with Indurain were Claudio Chiappucci, solid in second place, and Bugno, who led Hampsten by 2:51. Bugno trailed Hampsten by 2:02 and was in fifth place before the stage, the 19th of 21.

Bugno had dedicated his entire season to winning the Tour but rode like a bold champion only on the 64-kilometer (39-mile) individual race against the clock from Tours to Blois. Even then it was not quite good enough to threaten Indurain's dominance for more than half the course.

And what dominance he had shown. This was his sixth successive victory in long time trials in the last two Tours de France and the 1992 Giro d'Italia.

The Spaniard, riding elegantly, as always, finished in one hour 13 minutes 21 seconds. Bugno was 40 seconds slower after having trailed at nearly the halfway point by just one second. Dmitri Zhdanov, a Russian with Panasonic, was third, 2:28 behind Indurain. Looking extremely weary, Hampsten finished 27th, 5:33 behind. He led Pascal Lino, who was now in fifth place, by 57 seconds.

Indurain looked stylish in his yellow jersey and aero-dynamic Darth Vader helmet with built-in sun visor when he started down the Rue Nationale in Tours, crossed a bridge over the Loire and hung a right along the silted river.

Chiappucci, the only rider who had even a remote hope of overtaking the leader, left three minutes earlier and so the Spaniard knew the times of all his rivals.

A brisk tailwind pushed him along as he passed sandstone cliffs harboring caves where many people live, often in qualified splendor. Then Indurain swung inland, past the vineyards of Vouvray, a sparkling white wine, past fields of poppies, sunflowers or corn and through the Loire Valley countryside. At the first time check, kilometer 15 (mile 9) he was three seconds ahead of Bugno, with Hampsten third, 35 seconds down.

At kilometer 29, as the road still rose and fell gently, curving left and right regularly, Indurain was two seconds up and Hampsten had lost 1:18 to the second-placed Bugno.

Over the last half of the race, Indurain turned on the power and stretched his advantage. He was aided by the undemanding course, which required little technical skill but a lot of power. That Indurain certainly had.

With four kilometers (2.4 miles) to go, he spotted Chiappucci down the road and began trying to overtake him. He lost sight of the Italian only around curves and was targeting him for a flypast when the finish line ended the pursuit.

Chiappucci, who had been superlative in his constant attacks throughout the three-week race, deserved the dignity of not being overtaken. He finished with only seven seconds left of the three minutes he started before Indurain. And that was good enough for sixth place in the time trial. Any other time, it would have been quite a feat.

Lanterne Rouge

The last shall be first, they say, and for a brief moment in this Tour de France, Henri Manders was. First, that is. He had been last, or very near it, most of the rest of the time.

As the Tour neared its end the next day in Paris, Manders ranked 129th among the 130 riders remaining of the 198 who set out in Spain. He was nearly 15 minutes ahead of—or behind, depending on outlook—Fernando Quevedo in the battle to become the 79th Tour's lanterne rouge, the red lantern that used to hang on the back of every French train to signify the end.

Their status was unchanged after Stage 20, or 222 tedious kilometers (138 tedious miles) from Blois in the Loire Valley to Nanterre, just outside Paris.

Peter de Clercq, a Belgian with the Lotto team, won an eight-rider sprint finish, beating Flavio Vanzella, an Italian with GB-MG, and Thierry Laurent, a Frenchman with RMO. All ranked in the nether regions overall.

De Clercq was clocked in 6 hours 3 minutes 36 seconds, a leisurely pace on a torrid day. The main pack finished 7:31 behind the winner and Miguel Indurain remained unchallenged in the yellow jersey.

Manders and Quevedo finished in the same time with the main pack, changing nothing between them.

Their personal race was relatively tight until Stage 18, when Manders finished a splendid 10th into Tours while Quevedo was 130th and last, 7 minutes 21 seconds behind Manders. That doubled the Spaniard's deficit—or lead—in the fight to be lanterne rouge.

First things first: Manders, a 32-year-old Dutchman who rode for the Helvetia team from Switzerland, won a bonus sprint on July 20. Let the record show that his victory occurred in le Péage de Vizille, at kilometer 23 (mile 14) of the 15th stage, 198 kilometers from Bourg d'Oisans to St. Étienne, France.

Manders collected six bonus points in his total and 5,000 French francs (a bit less than $1,000). The money was the whole point of his bravado.

"I was in a group of 15 riders out ahead and I thought, 'Let's try to pick up some money to pay my fines that I got in the mountains,' " Manders said in an interview.

"When I won the sprint, I thought, 'Ah, my fines are paid'."

Then, zip! zip! zip! the rest of the breakaway passed Manders.

That was it for him as Numero Uno and he didn't care. Laurels are not accepted at the bank where fines are paid.

He declined to reveal how much he had been fined—"Not a lot"—presumably for accepting or soliciting uphill pushes from spectators.

There was not much else to talk about in the way of triumphs and Manders wore the look of a man who knew what was coming. He was in his seventh Tour de France and had finished the last three in 144th place, 113th place and 104th place. It was not significantly better before then, either.

How did it feel to be almost the lanterne rouge?

"Almost," he repeated emphatically. "It feels not so nice, no. It's not an honor any more."

There was a time, no more than a decade ago, when being the lanterne rouge was a highly publicized distinction. Riders actually slowed down to lose time and become the last man in the standings, knowing that they would be constantly interviewed and, because of the press coverage, would be invited to many of the criteriums in the Netherlands, Belgium and France that followed the Tour.

Those days were over, as much a part of the past as the entertainment the Tour used to provide after a daily stage.

A decade ago, the shows offered such attractions as Yvette Horner, the queen of the accordion, or a faded French chanteuse like Dalida. Now the entertainment was by a

British band dressed like the Blues Brothers, Jake and Elwood, and singing, quite terribly, Rolling Stones numbers.

Nor did a Tour employee still set up a movie projector to show flickering highlight films of past Tours on a wall in the village square. The highlights, without the shadows of moths in the projecter beam, were shown on nightly television now and the villages had mainly become ski resorts and big cities.

Now, also, the Tour organizers frowned on coverage about lack of success, like the lanterne rouge, feeling that it detracted from the leaders. And the criteriums were much reduced in number too.

Allan Peiper, a 32-year-old Australian who rode for Tulip and remembered the old days, had an added explanation.

"Nobody would try to become lanterne rouge now," he said. "It's too risky that you'd be outside the time limit" on a stage, while seeking to drop down, and would be eliminated.

Peiper had never been the lanterne rouge.

"But I've been pretty close every time, like I am now," he admitted. He ranked 124th overall.

"It doesn't matter. It used to be a bit of a novelty because the lanterne rouge was invited to all the criteriums, and now it's nothing. If you're last,… you're last. But last is better than fourth last, I suppose. The other end of the scale, you see."

Peiper was asked if there was any embarrassment in being last.

"No," he said. "These days, if you finish the Tour de France, if you're a bloody 20th or last, it's all the same. It's pretty hard, you know."

Manders agreed with that assessment but thought there was another reason that so few of the starters in Spain would finish.

"It used to be an honor to finish the Tour and I don't think today that riders race to finish. They want to win a stage and show themselves off."

He won a stage himself, in 1985.

"Seven years ago, yes," Manders said. "And I finished that Tour too.

"When I've finished this one, I've finished seven. And I've been in seven.

"It's not a record, of course, but I'm proud of it. Like everybody else, I've been quite sick sometimes, but I've always stayed in and finished the Tour de France." As he would the next day, and as Quevedo would too.

Last things last: Quevedo was a 27-year-old Spaniard with the Amaya team and was thrilled with his showing, he said.

"Last year, in my first Tour, I had to drop out with four stages to go. This year, I'll finish. Much better. Who cares if I'm last, I'm still in the Tour."

When he went to sign in for the stage, the Tour's announcer, the warm-hearted Daniel Mangeas, introduced him to the huge crowd of fans in Blois.

"Quevedo may be last," Mangeas declared, "but he'll be there on the Champs-Élysées tomorrow and he'll go back to Spain Monday on the same plane with Miguel Indurain. Think about that when you think of the lanterne rouge."

Quevedo, who understood French passably, thought about it himself and broke into a big grin.

The Winner and Still Champion

Looking to the manner born, Miguel Indurain rode regally into Paris as the winner of the Tour de France for the second successive year. Once again, it was not close.

Indurain finished the race 4 minutes 35 seconds ahead. His total time for the three-week, 3,983-kilometer (2,490-mile) ride through seven European countries was 100 hours 49 minutes 30 seconds.

Four and a half minutes may not sound like much of a drubbing of the 197 other riders who set out in San Sebastián, Spain in the 79th Tour de France, but it was at least that. Another description, less kind, was that he humbled his rivals.

They were the first to admit it.

"He was fabulous, overwhelming," said Andy Hampsten, who finished fourth overall.

Earlier in the race, Gianni Bugno, who finished third, likened the Spaniard to an extraterrestrial being for his speed and strength. Bugno was so despondent after he was crushed by Indurain in the first long time trial that he stopped seeing the sports psychologist who was trying to counsel him how to win the Tour.

"I intimidate my opponents," Indurain says rather hesitantly. His margin was 59 seconds bigger than the year before.

He accomplished that in a much tougher Tour than the 1991 edition, which was finished by 158 of the 198 starters. In 1992 only 130 out of 198 made it to Paris and none of the 22 teams saw all nine riders survive.

The dropouts were victims mainly of the rapid pace from the start. That same speed was maintained on the 141-kilometer (87-mile) 21st and final stage from the Alphaville complex of La Défense west of Paris out into the suburbs and then onto the Champs-Élysées for 10 laps of the broad avenue.

As usual, there were group and solo breakaways and, as usual, the Tour finished in a mass sprint. Olaf Ludwig, a German who rode for Panasonic, got his front wheel across the line first, edging Jean-Paul van Poppel, a Dutchman with PDM, and Johan Museeuw, a Belgian with Lotto. Ludwig's time, like everybody else's, was 3 hours 28 minutes 37 seconds.

And then the Tour was history.

As soon as Indurain headed for the victory podium to accept handshakes, kisses and a Sèvres vase, the celebrations began.

Thousands of Spaniards and Spanish Basques tore about, flapping their respective flags, and a French military band broke into the Spanish national anthem, which has no title. Indurain and his Banesto team also took a victory lap around the six-kilometer (3.7-mile) circuit of the Champs-Élysées. He was applauded most heartily by six busloads of fans from his village of Villava.

Other big winners included Claudio Chiappucci, who won the climbing title for the second successive year, and Laurent Jalabert, a Frenchman with ONCE, who won the points competition.

They got 512,500 and 500,000 French francs respectively, far below Indurain's 2 million francs (about $400,000) as the winner. The prizes are usually put in the team pool.

Chiappucci got 800,000 more francs for finishing second overall and Bugno got 300,000 for third place. The prizes totaled 10.1 million francs, or 1.47 million Ecus in Euro-speak.

Despite Indurain's dominance from the opening prologue to the second of two individual time trials, the Tour proved to be highly popular with fans. Crowds along the sides of the road in Spain, France, Belgium, the Netherlands, Germany, Luxembourg and Italy were vaster and more enthusiastic than they had been in recent years. The

Tour usually estimates spectator turnout at 15 million to 20 million.

Only the absence of hot, sunny weather during the first 10 days and in spots thereafter held down the fans and their cheering. Most of it was directed toward Indurain, and well it should have been. By the next Tour he would be 29 years old and still at his peak.

"Will he continue to be so dominant?" asked Raphael Géminiani, a former rider and directeur sportif. "How can you doubt it? He doesn't even know his limits yet."

Bernard Hinault agreed. "You can say that he won because of the time trials, but he was in command from the start. He dominates his era. If nobody attacks him in the Tour, he can do just what Anquetil, Merckx and I did: win it five times."

For his part, Indurain was making no predictions. Looking back over his victory, which he accomplished with a Tour record for the winner's speed at 39.5 kilometers an hour, he admitted, "There were risks and dangers every day, but I never doubted that I would win. It was a difficult Tour but I never had a difficult moment."

José-Miguel Echavarri, Banesto's directeur sportif and the man who knows Indurain best, was equally wary of predictions about five victories. "I said last year that I thought this was the first in a series for Miguel, but how many will be in that series? I don't know. Miguel isn't insatiable for victories but for doing the best that he can. That's why he was happy to finish second in the Vuelta" in 1991.

"He knows that at that time of the year, there are riders better than he is. If the public or the press wasn't happy with his second place, he was, because it was the best he could do.

"It's the same with the spring classics," Echavarri continued. Indurain rarely rides them, fearing that cold and rainy weather could undermine his health, and when he does enter a classic, he rarely does well.

"I'm sure that if he dedicated a season to winning classics, he would," Echavarri insisted. "But Miguel understands how cycling works and he knows that if a rider wins nothing but the Tour de France in a season, he's still the king." The king Indurain.

Getting Ready for the 80th Tour

When a rigorous and mountainous 1993 Tour de France was unveiled, the man with the big smile at the end of the presentation was Miguel Indurain. He smiles readily anyway, but he had special reasons to be pleased. The 80th edition of the Tour plays to the Spaniard's strengths: the long time trial and the high mountains.

The 1993 Tour listed three long time trials. The first, for full nine-man teams, will cover 85 kilometers (52.8 miles). The next two will be on an individual basis—along 65 kilometers for the first and along 55 kilometers for the second.

Between those two individual time trials come the mountains, lots of mountains. The first of two daily stages in the Alps will pass over three peaks. The next day will comprise four peaks, but not Alpe d'Huez, which has been dropped for the first time in a decade. The Pyrenees return to the Tour, with three stages to be held there. In all, Tour organizers listed 21 major climbs during the 3,800-kilometer, three-week race. Nine of these mountains tower more than 2,000 meters (6,600 feet), including such familiar terrain as the Galibier and Izoard Passes in the Alps and the Tourmalet Pass in the Pyrenees. The unfamiliar (not traversed by the Tour since 1964) Restefonds Pass in the Alps will be the peak at 2,802 meters.

Smaller but no less daunting will be the Glandon and Télégraphe Passes in the Alps and the Peyresourde and Aubisque Passes in the Pyrenees. All of them are standard Tour backbreakers.

"Lots of ups and downs," said Jim Ochowicz, general manager of the Motorola team based in the United States. "I don't think, though, it's harder than this year's Tour."

That was definitely a minority view.

"The course is a little bit frightening with so many mountains," said Indurain, failing to look frightened.

"It seems a lot harder, at least on paper," said Harrie Jansen, manager of the Buckler team, which will be sponsored now by WordPerfect.

"For sure more difficult," said Jan Gisbers, directeur sportif of PDM, which went out of existence at the end of 1992 as Gisberts moved to the Festina team.

"Much harder, and that last week will be a killer," said Maurice Le Guilloux, a former rider and directeur sportif.

The last week includes the visit to the Pyrenees and the final time trial, sandwiched around a long train trip from Bordeaux to the town of Brétigny, near Paris. The Tour will end in the capital with its traditional toing and froing on the Champs-Élysées.

It will start in the Vendée region of western France, specifically the town of le Puy du Fou. Unlike the 1992 edition, which visited seven European countries after starting in Spain, the 1993 Tour will cling to the motherland except for a sojourn to Andorra.

"That's a reaction to this year's route, when we were criticized for going abroad too much," said Jean-Marie Leblanc, the Tour's racing director, as he presented the itinerary.

Like a prisoner clawing at the walls, the Tour will cycle around the outer reaches of France, including Brittany, Normandy, the North, Lorraine, the southern Alps, the Mediterranean coast and the Atlantic coast. The heartland of the Massif Central, usually a pillar of the race, will be skipped.

As announced a year earlier, the field will be reduced from 22 nine-man teams to 20. The first 14 teams in the computerized rankings will gain automatic berths in May while 6 "wildcards" will be named in mid-June.

The reason for the reduction to 180 riders is basically safety. More and more of the secondary roads that the Tour uses have been modernized with traffic islands and other devices to limit carnage by French drivers, who rank among the world's bravest if not best.

Because of all the road impediments and its own nervous and rapid pace, especially in the dozen days of racing over flat stages, the Tour has found that the usual 198-man field is just too big to get out of its own way. The smaller field will lead to fewer crashes, officials hope.

The prize list will total 11 million francs with 2 million francs going to the winner. That announcement might have also contributed to Indurain's smile.

He had so much to be pleased with—his Giro and Tour victories, his marriage, his future—that not even his disappointing sixth place in the world championship road race, when Gianni Bugno retained the victor's rainbow-striped jersey, could keep the happiness off Indurain's face.

The First Lance

Finishing his first bicycle race as a professional by riding so far behind that he was alone, Lance Armstrong began thinking the unthinkable. "I thought maybe I wasn't any good," he said. "I thought, 'God, these guys are that much better than me.' It was very humbling."

Armstrong is not easily humbled. He is confident, articulate, likeable and, just 21 years old in mid-September 1992, one of the brightest prospects in the sport. But for a few weeks in the summer of that year he was simply another rider hunched over his handlebars, pumping his legs to no great, or even good, result. In a word, humbled.

As an amateur he was a favorite in the road race in the Olympic Games in Barcelona but finished 14th because, as he said, "I just didn't have the best legs. I had good legs but other guys had better legs."

A few weeks later, after he signed as a professional with the Motorola team, he was entered in his first race, the Clasica San Sebastián, a World Cup competition in Spain. The rainy weather was against him and so was the distance, 234 kilometers (146 miles), many more than he was accustomed to as an amateur. "It's tough when it's 250, 260 kilometers, but 200 I have no problem with," Armstrong said.

He finished 111th, dead last, 11 minutes behind the rider who was in 110th place. All alone as he plowed on, Armstrong refused to quit, as 95 of the 206 starters did. "It was my first race, my first professional race, and I didn't want to quit my first race," he explained. "I didn't want to finish but I didn't want to quit either."

Blooded in battle, he began to do well: a stage victory in the Tour of Galicia in Spain, second place in the Championship of Zürich, another World Cup race, and a victory in an Italian race. Then he finished 25th in the Tour de l'Avenir, the Tour of the Future, a French showpiece for young and promising riders.

Although Armstrong knew that Miguel Indurain and Greg LeMond both won the Tour de l'Avenir early in their careers and thus attracted their first broad attention, he was modest beforehand about his own goals in the race. "It's sort of preparation for the rest of the season, the remaining World Cup races," he said. "I'd like to have a stage win here. Definitely. That's a goal. But the overall classification, I have to see how it goes."

Despite his finish in general classification, his Motorola manager, Jim Ochowicz, was happy. "Lance is riding heads up and we're very pleased," he said. "He's definitely got a winning attitude. You don't have to motivate him."

In addition to attitude, Armstrong said, his form was good. "Good, but you never know, it comes and goes so quick. You get good form and there's that crest you have to hold and ride for as long as you can. It's pretty easy to go over it and start your descent." While his form held, however, Armstrong had a full racing schedule to finish the season: the Tour of Ireland and such World Cup races as the Grand Prix of Lombardy and the Grand Prix of the Americas in Montreal. "A lot of riding," he conceded, "but I'm begging for it."

He also had an inner schedule, and it called for him to be nothing less than a great star.

Armstrong has practiced and polished the line, used it in so many interviews now that his delivery is perfect. The straight man asks the inevitable question: Are you the next Greg LeMond? "No," he answers, "I'm the first Lance," (a healthy chuckle here for punctuation) "the first Armstrong."

It reads glibber than it sounds. The adjective often attached to Armstrong is "brash," but perhaps that's only his way of seeking self-protection. Speaking the Lance line, Armstrong can be understood to be asking for some breathing room, for respite against the LeMond comparison. Cut him some slack, as they say back home in Plano, Texas. He had just turned 21.

"I don't think it's fair to compare me to Greg LeMond," he said. "He's a great athlete and I think I'm a good athlete. Physically, we're a lot different," he continued. "He's a big guy (5 foot 10, 152 pounds) but he's not as big as me (6 foot 1, 180 pounds). Body type, there's no comparison. He turned pro when he was 19 but he also got married when he was 19, so I guess he started everything a little early."

Armstrong began competing on a bicycle at 12, "just to keep busy," but focused on many other sports first. "Being from Texas, of course I tried football, the mainstream sports thing, then tried swimming and got into triathlon from there and then got into cycling from there."

He is honest about why he changed sports. "I wasn't any good at football. No speed, no coordination." Swimming— 1,500 meters—was no different. "Again no speed," Armstrong says.

That analysis carries over to road racing. Asked to list his weaknesses, Armstrong said, "I don't have a lot of speed in cycling either. I'm not very quick in the sprint."

For his strengths, he named climbing and time trialing. Somewhere in between his strengths and weaknesses he put bike-handling skills. "They've improved greatly," he thought. "A lot of triathletes don't have very good bike-handling skills because they don't ride in packs."

Riding in packs offers other advantages, he continued, including the opportunity to compare himself directly to his opponents.

"The day that you're on, you're riding and you get this feeling that's like..." The words trailed off as Armstrong searched for a way to define ecstasy. "You're tired and you're hurting," he resumed, "but you just look around and you can tell that the guy next to you is hurting one notch more than you and you're recovering that much faster than him, and that's an incredible feeling."

Victory is another high. "When it's going good—I should say when you're winning—it's one of the most luxurious sensations. It's an incredible feeling to win major races, to come across with your hands in the air. It's like no other feeling in the world."

Victory matters a lot to Armstrong.

"I want to be a star," he said in an even voice.

"I know I want to do the Tour de France, I know I want to win the Tour de France. I think I can someday get to that level but that's a long way off, a lot of hard work. The desire is there, the ambition is there, the goal is there. It's only a matter of doing the hard work and winning the race.

"Everybody wants to win the Tour de France, everybody from Cat 4 up says, 'I want to win the Tour,' yet only one guy can win it each year," he continued. "LeMond has won it three times and look at his crowds, the way he's responded to. It's amazing.

"Win the Tour de France and you're a star. I'd like to be a star.

"I'm sure I'd get sick of all the pressure and all the appearances, but I'd like to try it for a while."

Other Titles Available from Bicycle Books

Title	Author	US Price
All Terrain Biking	Jim Zarka	$7.95
The Backroads of Holland	Helen Colijn	$12.95
The Bicycle Commuting Book	Rob van der Plas	$7.95
The Bicycle Fitness Book	Rob van der Plas	$7.95
The Bicycle Repair Book	Rob van der Plas	$9.95
Bicycle Technology	Rob van der Plas	$16.95
Bicycle Touring International	Kameel Nasr	$18.95
The Bicycle Touring Manual	Rob van der Plas	$16.95
Bicycling Fuel	Richard Rafoth	$9.95
Cycling Europe	Nadine Slavinski	$12.95
Cycling France	Jerry Simpson	$12.95
Cycling Kenya	Kathleen Bennett	$12.95
Cycling the U.S. Parks	Jim Clark	$12.95
In High Gear (hardcover)	Samuel Abt	$21.95
In High Gear (paperback)	Samuel Abt	$10.95
The High Performance Heart	Maffetone/Mantell	$9.95
Major Taylor (hardcover)	Andrew Ritchie	$19.95
The Mountain Bike Book	Rob van der Plas	$10.95
Mountain Bike Magic (color)	Rob van der Plas	$14.95
Mountain Bike Maintenance	Rob van der Plas	$9.95
Mountain Bikes: Maint. & Repair*	John Stevenson	$22.50
Mountain Bike Racing (hardcover)*	Burney & Gould	$22.50
The New Bike Book	Jim Langley	$4.95
Roadside Bicycle Repairs	Rob van der Plas	$4.95
Tour of the Forest Bike Race	H. E. Thomson	$9.95
Tour de France (hardcover)	Samuel Abt	$22.95
Tour de France (paperback)	Samuel Abt	$12.95

Buy our books at your local book shop or bike store.

Book shops can obtain these titles for you from our book trade distributor (National Book Network for the USA), bike shops directly from us. If you have difficulty obtaining our books elsewhere, we will be pleased to supply them by mail, but we must add $2.50 postage and handling (as well as California Sales Tax if mailed to a California address). Prepayment by check (or credit card information) must be included with your order.

Bicycle Books, Inc.
PO Box 2038
Mill Valley CA 94941
Tel.: (415) 381-0172

In Britain: Bicycle Books
463 Ashley Road
Poole, Dorset BH14 0AX
Tel.: (0202) 71 53 49

* Books marked thus not available from Bicycle Books in the UK